Permission To Speak

GODFREY TALBOT

Permission To Speak

Hutchinson of London

Hutchinson & Co (Publishers) Ltd
3 Fitzroy Square, London W1

London Melbourne Sydney Auckland
Wellington Johannesburg and agencies
throughout the world

First published September 1976
Second impression April 1977
© Godfrey Talbot 1976

Set in Monotype Garamond
Printed in Great Britain by litho at
The Anchor Press Ltd and bound by
Wm Brendon & Son Ltd, both
of Tiptree, Essex

ISBN 0 09 127250 5

To the memory of Richard

Contents

Illustrations

In the Text

I

Menu

I have been having an affair with a microphone for forty years. A professional relationship with love in it.

Of course, there have been times when I have hated the wretched device that I lived with; times when I was quite tired enough and quite overburdened enough without having to cart the mike and the tape-recorder in and out of planes and cars and radio studios; and times of absolutely hating the technical demands of the thing at my lips. But mostly it has been a cherished partner, an instrument of achievement, deliverer of bread-and-butter. Second nature to talk to it, bereavement to be without it, a prolonged kiss of life to a broadcaster on the move: the microphone, my dear.

Born of this implement, my business has been words, words spoken and widely heard. The business still goes on, officially retired though now I am from the staff of the best-known broadcasting organization in the world (because of the accident of my date of birth). I find myself still talking professionally and in public both by radio as a freelance and by appearance before visible audiences as a speaker at conferences and classes, luncheon-club meetings and assorted dinners. Lecturing, they call this, but wrongly in my case: the word suggests donnish discourses, whereas most of my public speaking, though it deals in instant history, is about people and places and the trials of travel, the very personal and sometimes eccentric adventures I have had as an authorized busybody. What is usually asked of me at the gatherings in the Masonic halls and grand hotels is the human picture, the close-up view and the peep behind the scenes of great events. So it is 'I

Was There at the Time' and 'Face to Face with the Famous'.

But spoken commentary, whether it is delivered to seen or unseen hearers, is a continual will-o'-the-wisp, forceful but fleeting. The words and the sounds escape. Quite often I have not been particularly proud of what I have said, glad that it has all flown off into the void forever, hopeful that BBC Sound Archives had not recorded the stuff on transmission; but on the occasions when I have enjoyed doing a broadcast or a talk, and have felt that it passed muster, I have regretted the ephemeral nature of my profession's output and wished that it might have some substance and permanence. I wanted to keep the off-the-record tales too.

Therefore this book.

Before my memories are sunk beneath the surly advance of decrepitude I am going to impound a few of them here. I am certain that I shall miss the aid of voice and gesture, the telling pause and suggestive intonation, the expressive wave of a hand and lift of an eyebrow; I shall not have an audible laugh and an observable shrug to gloss over my inadequacies. The book may well be like Talbot talking palely. Still, I have written before and I am now deliberately seeking the comfort of the printed page and its permanent outlines as I write down words instead of saying them.

Write down what?

Echoes, lots and lots of echoes: recollections that are both mine and my generation's. Adventures in tearing round the world with a radio commentator's permission to speak from the scenes of news; reporting from the spot. Beginnings have to be in the tale too: the magic of broadcasting in its infancy in the days when there was some wonder and grace and respect in life – the early twenties (how strange it sounds in the present ugly and cynical age to recall that people used to stand up when they heard the National Anthem on the wireless; that men took their hats off when they passed the Cenotaph in Whitehall, even when they passed it sitting in a bus). My own fixation with the business of broadcasting even before I went into newspapers and long before I joined the exclusive BBC – that must be part of the story too. And experiences at the front (and the rear) as a war correspondent; what I saw later when

travelling abroad with the Royal Family; and not forgetting
the backstage whimsies inside the studios as well as the on-
stage wonders on the streets of ceremonial London. No doubt
some of the tricks of the trade will become exposed.

Another thing about the contents of this memorial of mine
is that, like the famous memorial which David Copperfield's
Mr Dick was forever writing, mine will unquestionably have
its own King Charles's Head coming persistently into it. But
I shall encourage its entrances into the story, for the head
in my case is Winston Spencer Churchill, whose figure, greater
than a king's, bulks with considerable majesty into the years
I have known.

I shall not be able to help demonstrating an affection for
small things and lighter moments. There is great sorrow and
dark loss enough in the world – and in my own private world –
without my dilating on tragedy. In any case, one of the bless-
ings of memory is that we tend to fade and relegate the heavy
days and harsh encounters but retain, clear and sharp in the
mind, the occasions that were fun, the entertaining times when
we laughed and found kindness and success. Certainly my own
recollections are unashamedly partial to the illuminating off-
beat details which for me have made great events fascinating
and which – especially the mishaps sometimes – have brought
life and great humanity to pasteboard performances.

So you will have no horrendous wartime battle stories from
me. Not even a recall of my grimmer assignments of what we
call peacetime – like the railway accidents, the Aberfan ava-
lanche, France's Algerian terror years, or those grievous days
back in 1948 when I stood on the ravaged docksides of Hamburg and watched the bloody disembarking of immigrant
Jews turned back from their Promised Land of Palestine: a
shrieking episode which sickened me more than anything I
saw during the war. No, this story is about pleasanter moments.

You will find that there is a great deal about radio and relatively little about television. This is not to deny the ascendancy of picture over word in the communication of news;
nor is it to overlook that I have experience of television performance. I do not favour radio just because it is now a
Cinderella coming out from a spell in the kitchen and going

to the ball, either. The truth is that I like the old medium, always have done, and so have worked a great deal in Sound. What is more, I confess to liking to turn my back nowadays on the TV screen's displays of violence and its powerful highlighting of destruction in particular and immorality in general, which I well know to be born of the editors' eternal lust for exciting film in the name of news. Whereas radio – much as I loathe the destructive interview and the demented 'pop' muzak which is not the food of love to me – is not so upsetting, so searing, so over-simplifying or so dramatizing a communicator, and not so likely to spark imitations of law-less acts reported. Radio has, on the whole, more decency, more intelligence and more civilized gentleness in the manner of its treatment of current affairs.

If that reads like an echo of Mesdames Grundy and White-house, so be it. My book will have certain disinterested ani-mosities in it, and I mean to take my prejudices for an airing.

All the same, I shall probably be insistently cheerful most of the time. You will not get a repeating groove of Ichabod. Evocation of Those Good Old Days, certainly, but no cry of All is Lost. I am too fascinated by life – even life in this age of long hair and short views – for anything of that sort; and anyhow I never have and never do come back from doing a broadcast without some redeeming hilarity to tell. Nobody collects Auntie's bloomers more keenly than I (though since the BBC isn't very Auntie now we may need another *mot* for speakers' howlers), and the old spoonerisms still give joy: the piece of music announced as 'The Bum of the Flightlebee', the princess wearing an 'off-the-hat-face', the sporting com-mentary foretold as being on 'the hearse racing from Horst Park,' and the Royal Yacht *Gothic* coming out as 'the Royal Clot Yothic'. I love the funnies.

You cannot, thank God, be brought up in the North of England, as I was, without having a saving sense of humour. It is something which goes with and leavens the bluntness practised north of the River Trent. I believe that some in-heritance of that combination of drollery and directness helps in broadcasting. It makes for straightforwardness: in my Yorkshire they have a habit of seeing through pretension and ridiculing fancy behaviour pretty quickly; artful fabrications are smartly spotted and demolished, so the person who tries those tricks is often shamed into sincerity. Such purging is good medicine if you are going to talk professionally, for if you have had a dose or two already you are less likely to have to be stiffly physicked when on the job, less prone to be discouraged or rejected in your first essays in broadcasting and encounters with the microphone, your highly critical instrument of broadcasting. The microphone itself is a very good examiner and editor, and it is fatal to treat it with disrespect, even when it has been your paramour over the years. It has a peculiar way of discovering and exposing artificiality for what it is. It is more than a servant: it is a sieve. Beware it.

Well!

I must myself beware – of sounding as though I am the most self-satisfied and pedantic pontificator this side of the Urals. I hope that the confessions which follow will remove any such impression: I intend not to write a treatise but to switch some sidelights on to a public profession. To do this I shall employ as best I can a long but fallible memory, hoping that inevitable errors and omissions, which are my own and no one else's, will be found bearable and pardoned.

But enough of menu; let's start the meal. Off with the prologue and on with the piece.

Once upon a time . . .

2

On the Wireless

When I joined the BBC the Reith of respectability still lay
monumentally upon the public air, though it was the last year
of Sir John's reign. In 1937 the wireless was soberly decorous
and spoke grave English. The Director-General saw to that.
Quality and dignity were taken for granted.

That, as a matter of fact, was why the British Broadcasting
Corporation and its servants were in a state of shock when I
arrived. Auntie had hiccoughed. The famous 'Fleet's lit up'
broadcast had happened a few days before I became one of the
staff, and as I walked into Broadcasting House the place was
still alight with the shame and flame of it. Celebrations of the
Coronation of the new king, George the Sixth, were taking
place that year. As part of them, the might of the Royal Navy
was assembled at Spithead for a mammoth review; and one
night the BBC broadcast, 'live', a description of the illumination of the Fleet by Lieutenant-Commander Thomas Woodrooffe, a popular, very able, and at that period very overworked
commentator. On that night he was liberally entertained
aboard his old ship before the hour of his commentary; and
when he began to speak it was clear that he, as well as the
assembled Fleet, was illuminated. So, in the event, the description did not last very long, for Tommy Woodrooffe for
once was not coherent. London faded him out; and the lapse
became a national sensation.

What a thing to happen in that correct, paternalistic world
of the British wireless! Here was Sir John Reith's mighty
Corporation being much less than correct. Here was Auntie
BBC suddenly fallible and human. The listeners tittered and

the Press trumpeted, alike entranced. There was much tut-tutting and disapproval too. No one belonging to the present permissive age, no one who was not a listener forty years ago, can imagine the fuss. Inside the Corporation there was hardly any topic of conversation save Tommy's utterances and the public axing of them. The official inquest on the incident went on for days; it was protracted because most of broadcasting's hierarchy had been guests aboard ships at Spithead that night and had not even heard the broadcast. It was, moreover, a post-mortem behind closed doors. The importunate newspapers, dying to know what really happened at the microphone aboard the battleship *Nelson*, were told only that there had been 'technical difficulties'. Tommy didn't talk, and all the Corporation said was that he had been suspended for six weeks. In those days BBC officials tended to be upstage characters who didn't pander to unsavoury people like reporters. They were nervous about journalists and few knew much about them. The newspapers' importance was beginning to be realized, but their outside staffs were looked upon as riff-raff by the boss class in Broadcasting House.

Such an attitude, and such an occurrence as the Woodrooffe Affair, made my first days as a Corporation Man difficult. For I was a reporter myself – was newly hired as one, in fact. I had been recruited as a BBC Public Relations Officer, a link between the Corporation and the world around it, a spokesman to answer inquiries and indeed to vouchsafe snippets of news to the Press, a licensed tattler among tight-lipped men. In those days it was a new sort of job.

From daily journalism in Manchester I had applied for the advertised post of Press Officer, North Region, a new appointment which was an earnest of the Corporation's effort to be less aloof and more professional. Auntie was recruiting a few Players to mix with the Gentlemen.

The old order seemed still to be prevailing, though, when I went up to London to face an appointments board in an oak-panelled courtroom deep inside Broadcasting House. I had been short-listed for the job and was summoned for an interview. It felt more as though I was up for a criminal trial when I entered the room and was bidden to sit down in front

17

of a long table on the other side of which were six solemn men, each looking either bristlingly Service or banefully academic. They were a retired proconsul, a man from the Civil Service, the BBC appointments officer, a regional director, the programme controller and a staff manager appositely named St John Pym. An awe-inspiring lot. Nobody there, it appeared, who knew about publicity and newspapers – or me. They shuffled papers and with patent effort asked irrelevant questions like 'Are you musical at all?' and 'D'yer play cricket?' and 'What *are* your games, Mr . . . er, Talbot, isn't it?' The former Empire-builder looked down his nose and said, disparagingly, 'I see you went to a grammar school.' Then, trying to make amends, he put *both* feet in it, adding, 'We know it takes all sorts to make a world.'

After a while one of the inquisitors gave up and left the room, walking out as though he had taken too much liquid aboard at lunch – though I heard later that he had gone to telephone the Manchester office to ask if anybody had heard of me. The other five ran out of talk then, and I was asked to summarize my career. In spite of knowing that they had it on my application form in front of them, I reviewed myself as best I could. Next, the Civil Service man pulled himself together and kept the ball rolling with: 'Why do you want to get into the BBC? Are you unhappy?' When I had dealt with that one there came more quizzing about my family background, my recreations, my religion. Nothing about my press cuttings. Then, finally, a fairly bleak thank-you-we'll-let-you-know, and out I went, feeling small, through a waiting-room full of other applicants, all obvious games players who'd been to the right schools.

But you never can tell. A few days later, shortly before the Coronation, came a letter saying I was the one who had been chosen. They hoped I would accept the offer of the post, on six months' probation, and that I would report to my base, North Regional headquarters in Manchester, on 7 June. I accepted.

So it was in my native North that I began my long years in broadcasting. But not, then, as a public talker. Just a PRO. But fortunately my public relations work in the first few days in June 1937 was concerned with our Northern programmes, not with Commander Woodrooffe, so I did not have to try to answer my old newspaper friends' questions about the still-burning topic of the light and darkness of the fleet. I referred all inquiries about Spithead to London.

Before many months had passed I was hauled up to London myself. I shall not forget first walking into Broadcasting House, the new building in Portland Place. In those days the entrance hall was like a lofty temple emblazoned with Latin inscriptions about Johannes Reith and nation speaking peace unto nation and equipped with huge flower vases and receptionists in immaculate black. The atmosphere of the place was so chaste that I felt I was about to take Holy Orders. I was certainly about to take BBC orders, for I had been ordered to the Staff Training School. They wanted me to learn about the total Corporation, not merely my provincial part of it. Three whole months they kept me at school at headquarters. I thought it too long for my indoctrination, and said so. But I was told that Manchester could well get along without me for a bit: I had started well enough – that was the way it was put – and our Lancashire and Yorkshire programme output was really getting more than its share of fame. What it amounted to was that London was jealous of the very lively broadcasting in North Region.

The training school at that time was new and small, its courses attended by only about twenty men and women each term – an assortment of producers, music and talks assistants, Children's Hour organizers, administrators and engineers. We learned about each others' jobs. We sat through weeks of lectures on every section of the Corporation's activities, and then everybody had a go at giving talks and producing feature programmes. I was reckoned fairly good at doing funny dialect voices in plays, but not distinguished at anything else. However, I learned much about who was who and what was what in the mighty microcosm for which I worked. I liked noseying into other people's departments and I was encouraged to do this. After all, I was 'a BBC spokesman', at any rate to the Press.

Even though I watched and listened with the professional

suspicion of an investigating newsman, I began to find much to admire and be proud of in the things the BBC was doing; and I must say my student days were agreeable, leisurely and desultory compared to the concentrated slog of the very businesslike courses which are run by the Corporation nowadays. The pace of the lessons was easy, the personnel at the school variegated.

Though the chief instructor knew broadcasting thoroughly (he was Archie Harding, a brilliant pioneer producer and a one-man forcing house of radio talent), the Head of School during my term was not noticeably qualified, except perhaps as an arbiter of punctuality and polished shoes. He was a scrubbed and straightforward naval captain, good and guileless, a kindly jingo whom only a churl would dislike. Ignorance of the mechanics of radio and its programmes did not prevent him from enjoying his position. At every opportunity he would leave his cabin (that is what he called it though it was the school's administration office to landlubbers and other ordinary people) to sit with us in the classroom during playbacks and the discussions which followed them. He would air his personal phobias freely, contradicting skilled tutors in a voice suggesting that he was still abaft the mainmast and laughing so immoderately that he often fell to the floor from his extravagantly tilted chair.

It was an age when 'the Corp' was full of quirky characters (heaven knows, it is today, but now they tend to be the untidy, anarchical kind). Some were frank teachers of morals, some tireless chauvinists. The firm seemed to be run by talented amateurs; but they were a dedicated *corps d'élite*. As to the programmes, they were very consciously responsible – and on Sundays downright dull (half our listeners fled to Radio Luxembourg each Sabbath). The radio output took its tone and independence from the Director-General himself, a stranger character than any playwright would dream of inventing.

I met Reith face to face only once. He strode into the room fierce-eyed and disapproving, vain and craggy and curt, reminding me, for all his long pin-striped legs and shaven chin, of a spiteful Old Testament prophet. He looked at my Weekly

Notes for the Press with distaste and went off into a tirade about godless editors he knew. As other members of staff came in and the audience was better, he slid into a series of unappreciative comments about politicians and what he would do with them; and he certainly had a prophet's zeal and fire.

It was the six-feet-six-inches of John Reith's austere character and North British snobbery rather than his war-scarred face which made Winston Churchill call him 'Old Wuthering Heights'. Churchill's abomination of Reith was profound but was nothing compared to Reith's venomous loathing of Churchill. The two antagonists had some similar qualities, when you come to think of it. Each was innately impatient with egalitarian democracy, and each was out of touch with the man in the street.

Reith's influence pervaded every BBC studio centre in the land. It made the office atmosphere of my early days on the staff feel staid after the scramblings of life in a newspaper building. My secretary used to look pained whenever I said 'damn' or worked with my jacket off and my braces showing.

All the same, in the North Region we were not so stuffy as London. We didn't deal too much with solemnities and proprieties, though we had a pride in high standards. I was happy in my new work, very happy indeed; happy that at last I had got into the broadcasting business. The BBC, which through the years was to become my education, had long been my ambition.

As a boy in Leeds in the 1920s, straining to hear the early sounds of radio through the squeaky oscillations of a crystal set which looked like a canary's cage, I had become hooked on The Wireless. With hands pressing the earphones to my head I listened-in for hours. The addiction even interfered with my visits to the Headingley ground to watch our invincible Yorkshire eleven and to hang adoringly round the pavilion to get the autographs of Hirst and Sutcliffe, Rhodes and Kilner and other flannelled professionals who were the gods of the North, where cricket was a religion; it stopped my hours of lone bowling practice at a set of wickets I used to plant in the hen-run at the side of our house. It estranged me a little from my Methodist family and reduced my attendances at chapel – though I do remember that it was coming home from morning service one Sunday that I met a man, a friend of Father's, who had actually spoken on the BBC. That was an excitement. It made the chap very special in my eyes, a new kind of god, albeit a god in an old grey Homburg hat and the kind of celluloid wing-collar we used to call a come-to Jesus when Father wasn't hearing. Once, too, I got inside the Leeds studio. Station 2LS it was, in a converted house in Woodhouse Lane, the inside walls all padded and curtained till all the sound was dead. There, indeed, I first laid eyes upon the gently elegant Philip Fox, 'Leeds Representative', who for forty years was to preside over the destinies of the BBC in the city with a smiling grace which always suggested that he had simply looked in for a glass of sherry and had nothing to do with programmes. And as a matter of fact for most of his career he hadn't. A charming man, though: real old BBC.

I hankered after being in radio even at school and as the years went on and I became a newspaper man, a young editor – I ran the *Manchester City News* at the age of twenty-four – and a writer on the *Yorkshire Post* and the old *Daily Dispatch*. The BBC to me was special. But it was those very early broadcasting times, the early twenties, which thrilled most. No subsequent marvels, not even the wonder of colour television four decades later, have matched the first chirpings of Sound. It is not possible for today's generation, blasé about the Transistor and the Box, stereo and satellite, to imagine how novel it all was, how miraculous to hear Big Ben without being in London (BBC engineers captured the sound of the famous strokes by putting a carbon microphone inside a football bladder placed up in the clock tower at Westminster).

When Manager Reith in the very early days invited the Archbishop of Canterbury and his lady to listen to the wireless, Dr Davidson could only say, 'I'm thunderstruck!' His wife asked the engineer if it would be possible to listen-in without the window being open.

Even the thirties, when I became part of broadcasting, were exciting pioneer years when remembered today. But radio had grown fast. It was nation-wide, no longer a novelty but an accepted part of everyday life. There was a loudspeaker in most homes, bringing to British firesides as familiar friends the voices (though not, until wartime, the names) of Stuart Hibberd, Freddie Grisewood, Frank Phillips and Alvar Lidell. On foreign affairs the universal authorities were Vernon Bartlett and Stephen King-Hall; and there was a worshipped Gardener of the Air named Mr Middleton – possibly the best natural broadcaster there has ever been, though I must say there is something about horticulture which propagates lovely warm voices in any era, for the sound of Messrs Loads, Gemmell and Sowerbutts in 'Gardeners' Question Time' takes some beating.

The BBC Symphony Orchestra was firmly established in the thirties, and so was the dance band of Henry Hall. A comedian called Handley was even then a name: Tommy was paid a whole ten guineas for each broadcast.

Such was the output from London. But my own concern, up in Manchester, was with the Northern programmes and the Northern people. I was fortunate to begin my BBC career with a vintage Manchester staff; lucky to learn from the shrewd programme director, John Salt; from the poet, John Pudney; from Geoffrey Bridson, the Corporation's most talented feature writer ever; and especially from a fiercely uncompromising talks editor, Donald Boyd, apostle of the spoken word, discoverer and moulder of good broadcasters, the man who was to forge the BBC's pioneer techniques of war reporting (how I wish Donald was alive today to demolish the kind of radio reporting that is doughy and dead with the print-clichés of journalese).

North Regional radio output gave me a richness of programme material to publicize: Victor Smythe's ebullient shows from the old Argyll Theatre in Birkenhead, for instance, and his Outside Broadcast jamborees in the Isle of Man each June when the TT motor-cycle races were on – and when our commentators and engineers, splendid lusty characters, savoured highway broadcasts and hotel bars with equal zest and hardly went to bed for a week. We had first-class concerts, and the best Children's Hour in the country. The Hour included a regular and enormously popular country-walks-with-a-gipsy feature, 'Out with Romany', spoken with mellow naturalness by a certain Reverend Bramwell Evens, whose performances were in fact scripted and delivered entirely from inside the Manchester studios but were delivered with such windswept informality – and such expert sound effects – that listeners couldn't but believe that the broadcasts came from the open countryside. Evens threw himself into the programme so enthusiastically that he would at times abandon his type-written brief and wander round the studio – with the effects boy chasing him and pulling him back to the microphone stand.

Romany used to have with him on his walks a couple of youngsters. Actually, they were not children; they were two of the Aunties of our Children's Hour, Muriel and Doris, who with the greatest of ease and charm were able to make their voices and manner sound exactly like ten-year-old girls. Those two, Muriel Levy and Doris Gambell, took part in almost everything which North Region put out: actresses, writers and songbirds they were, exceptionally talented. Muriel was a first-class script writer and adapter, Doris the possessor of one of the purest soprano voices I have ever heard. For years the pair of them were two-thirds of a lively singing trio called The Three Semis which broadcast frequently. Their partner was another regular radio person called Violet Carson, a smartly dressed and most attractive Lancashire girl, smiling and beautifully spoken, who played the piano too. I still find it incredible and somehow contrary to nature that this is the Miss Carson who is famous today, decades later, as the old harridan Ena Sharples in commercial television's 'Coronation Street'. A good actress and kindly person, Violet is as sweet as Ena is sour.

Another name well known then, and still in business, is Wilfred Pickles. He too was in Manchester, a character actor first, then compère and announcer. A very useful general purposes man to have around in the studios, a good mixer, a bright talker, never off-balance. Or hardly ever. I do re-member one night when his jaw dropped and no word came out. We were doing a big feature programme by Bridson about Life in the Pennine towns. Many Yorkshire and Lancashire men and women were taking part in it, as well as radio actors and singers and our own Northern Orchestra. There was also a brass band, a choir, and groups of mill workers and house-wives. A real houseful: every part of Manchester's Broad-casting House was packed. The amateur performers arrived in the late afternoon in two coachloads, and came surging through the BBC door in Piccadilly. Soon they were busy rehearsing. So many people were in the production that you saw only the performers who occupied the particular studio you happened to be in: each studio, and the various speakers and musicians, were 'mixed' by the producer at a remote control-panel, and Wilfred Pickles was in the announcer's cubicle to speak the narration which linked them all.

After two hours of rehearsal there came a short but welcome interval before the transmission of the show. During this break Wilfred was standing in a corridor crowded with performers having a longed-for smoke. He turned to chat with a small, middle-aged man squashed beside him:

"Ow do? Which part are you in, then? Have you got one of t'speaking parts, happen?'

The reply was non-committal: 'Nay, lad, not me.'

'So which lot – a bandsman, mebbe?' countered Wilfred.

'Never!'

'The clog dancer then?'

'Don't be daft.'

'You must be with the Hebden Bridge Party.'

'Weere's Hebden Brig? No!'

Wilfred confessed that there were so many folk in the programme that he couldn't really tell t'other from which; and he then hoped the man really would tell him just what he was doing in the show. But the man only said:

'That's reet. Must be difficult.' He rubbed the back of his neck and gazed round at the throng. 'It's a grand experience. Allus wanted to see inside this place.'

Wilfred couldn't help trying again, and said: 'This must be a change from working in the mill.'

'Ah've nowt to do wi' mills.'

'Then I've got it,' said Wilfred. 'You must be the Oldham lamplighter who comes in early in the show.'

'Nay!'

'Then you're the knocker-up who wakes people for early shifts?'

'Nowt o't soort!'

It now seemed to Mr Pickles that the conversation had reached the stage where guessing-games were no longer either useful or amusing, so he asked simply: 'What section of the programme *do* you belong to?'

At this, the man confessed: he belonged nowhere; he was a stowaway! He had been standing at the end of the bus-stop queue on the pavement near the Broadcasting House entrance and had got in the way of one of the disgorging coachloads of performers making for the studios. He found himself swept along in the jostling stream and, detached from the bus queue, precipitated inside the BBC doorway whence our commissionaire on duty hurried him and everybody else inside. Nothing loath, curious and in no hurry, the stranger allowed himself to be hustled up to the studios with the rest. Nobody had questioned him until now.

Wilfred listened to the man's tale with astonishment and roared with laughter. So where, he asked, had the visitor been during the last two hours of rehearsing? The answer left our voluble announcer momentarily speechless:

'Ah've bin in t'big room – singing wi' t'choir.'

The man was allowed to stay – *and* to sing. It was something that could only have happened in the North.

It would not have happened even there if any of our administrative chiefs had been around the studios in Manchester that night. Rules and traditions, proprieties and protocol were stressed to the staff by senior executives. As a new boy, I had to learn to mind my p's and q's and to remember that the local hierarchy counted little things important. One day I committed the sin of sitting in the absent Regional Director's chair at one of the daily rituals of afternoon tea in the boardroom. There was a swift intake of breath round the table; and later I was taken aside by the oldest admin hand and quietly reprimanded. He made me feel that I had done my prospects in the Corporation no good at all, expecially as I had blotted my copybook in another way the week before when I played in a staff cricket match and ran out the Chief Executive, who

liked to think he was a good batsman and was very cross with
me.

I need not have worried about the Regional Director himself being cross, though. *He* would not have minded if he had
found me perched in his chair at teatime. For that particular
boss of mine was not the usual BBC type. John Coatman was
his name, and at that time he was new in the Northern post.
He had been sent up to be our chief after a spell as nominal
Editor of the BBC's embryonic news unit in London, whose
work was to write broadcast bulletins, for the announcers to
read out, from the messages sent in on the news-agency tape
machines. Before that, he had been an officer in the Indian
police and a professor at the London School of Economics. He
had no experience of professional journalism – his appointment
as News Editor was typical of the amateur-gentleman way the
Corporation was run in Reith's days – and had only whimsical
ideas of broadcasting. Or so we thought at first. John Coatman
liked to behave as an unlettered farmhand, which he certainly
was not. He was a bluff father figure, a man of channelled
enthusiasms – for anything regarding the county of Lancashire,
for instance. Chunky, with unkempt but close-cropped hair,
untidily dressed, he used to roll down the corridor from his
office like some primitive creature walking on the outsides
of its feet. He carried his head on one side and habitually had a
foul pipe in his mouth. He liked his pint of ale as well as his
baccy, and he liked to air his forthright views. He smiled
readily, he liked almost all people and almost everybody liked
him. He stirred the Region with some extraordinary programme ideas from time to time, but for the most part he left
the bothersome minutiae of broadcasting to his staff – which
left him free to be busy with interests of his own and pursuits
of his past.

One day I drove him to North Wales to attend the funeral
of a member of the staff who had died suddenly after long years
of service. What might have been a solemn journey was with
John Coatman a hilarious one. He sat beside me talking away
like a schoolboy on an outing. He reminisced, cracked jokes,
gave a running commentary on the passing scenery ('Nice
to see a bit of arable – oh, and there's a great sow got loose

27

in the vegetables'), and encouraged me to talk about my own upbringing in peggy-tub Yorkshire. He littered the floor of the car with half-spent matches because he was forever failing to light his pipe, he waved vigorously to passers-by, and occasionally looked down and turned the pages of a large book which he carried on his lap. He said it was an excellent story and he would let me read it later – and then he at once rumbled with laughter at his own joke, for the book was in Baluchi, a language in which Coatman was an examiner during his service on the Indian frontier. When we got to the village of our destination he insisted on going into a pub for what he described as a quick lunch which turned out to be hunks of cheese and pints of beer. He enjoyed this so much, as well as half an hour of loud exchanges with assembled Welsh miners and farmhands, that we arrived at the little chapel of the funeral awfully late and all astumble over the feet of the family mourners as we took our reserved places in a front pew.

He was forgiven. You could not help forgiving him. In his own disarming way, Honest John was a great charmer. An attractive teddy-bear of a person, a scholar playing the bucolic.

But we were living in unattractive times. Gay company though there was in Manchester's Broadcasting House, it was the defiant gaiety of the ball in Brussels on the eve of Waterloo. The late thirties were the last years of peace. You had only to twiddle the knobs of your radio set to realize that. Whilst the BBC programmes radiated fun and goodwill, nasty noises dominated the air on the other side of the Channel where powerful German stations carried the screaming threats of a hell-bent Hitler. War was certainly coming. Even before 1938 and Chamberlain's Munich sell out we were attending lectures on air raids and civil defence. We in the BBC had been privily told which parts of the kingdom various sections of the Corporation would disperse to when the balloon went up; and, like many members of the staff, I carried in my wallet secret orders telling me what I must do and where I must go on emergency duty when war broke out.

So it was that September 1939 found me translated to London. My National Service instructions laid down that I must remain with the BBC but must report for duty in the central, and now all-important, News Room at our head-quarters. After little more than two years of cosy playing at public relations, I was back to the job in which I had had years of hard practice: it was a return to my proper profession, news journalist. And now dealing with the sternest possible news. I was still a writer, not yet a speaker myself but one of a team of sub-editors whose duty was to write the wartime bulletins which announcers read whilst the whole nation listened.

I had left my family up in Lancashire, and was myself billeted in London by the BBC. And what a billet! I was quartered in the Langham Hotel in Portland Place, just across the road from BH – 'The Langham', grandest of all the Grand Hotels of Victorian London. The BBC had seized that vast palace for its 'essential staff' to sleep in during the first months of the emergency. Never had there been such luxurious dormitories. My own chamber was awe-inspiring. In the intervals between intensive shift work I retired to bed in an ornate and lofty suite complete with ambassadorial audience room.

Later, the Langham was permanently taken over by the Corporation as one of a cluster of BBC office buildings, but during the war it remained a kind of hotel annexe to Broadcasting House. And, like BH, it was damaged by air-raid bombing. When a land mine fell in Portland Place one particularly hideous night in the 1940 Blitz the explosion tore holes in the building. The walls stood up to the shock extraordinarily well, but much damage was done by flooding from the thirty-eight-thousand-gallon roof-top water tank which in the old days had been the hotel's special pride. I remember being out in the street and wondering where on earth the lake was coming from – for there wasn't a fire hose in sight just then – as I sloshed and crunched around in a road-way which had become filled with a kind of soup compounded of water and stones and broken glass.

In the raids of 1940 our News Room was moved three floors below ground in the bowels of Broadcasting House, alongside the main control room which had gone below from the eighth floor (when BH was built this vital operating centre was a roof-top department – and so of course was most vulnerable in war). The News Room was hot and crowded, but safe and satisfactory. The studio where the bulletins were actually read was right alongside us. Such proximity was admirable, but there was a snag. Like the News Room, the studio was reasonably bomb-proof but not absolutely sound-proof; and sometimes the listeners to the news could hear Bakerloo Line tube trains rumbling along their tunnel not very far below us. We also had a rather makeshift studio for the after-the-News talk, and this had a lavatory next door, a loo with what I can only describe as orchestral plumbing. During talks we had to station a copy-boy outside the door to make sure that nobody went in and flushed the very audible W C.

There was more than a lavatory to guard, of course. Broadcasting House was a nerve centre of a nation at war, and the News Room was its vitals. Home Guards protected us day and night. B H had become bricked-up, sandbagged and camouflaged. From outside the place looked like a great grey battleship pointing down to Oxford Circus. The entrance hall, a calm temple of flowers no longer, resembled a wire-fenced guardroom in which khaki men carrying bayoneted rifles stood beside steel pill-boxes and challenged each arrival at the doors.

Our famous announcers were a changed sight too. Far from wearing dinner jackets and boiled shirts to read the Nine o'Clock News, it was now jerseys and sports coats, flannel bags and shirt sleeves; and there were bulletins to read at all sorts of hours from seven in the morning till midnight.

Naturally enough, the very early shift saw the most careless attire, but occasionally undress was overdone. The announcer on early-morning duty used to sleep in the building, ready on hand to read the breakfast-time bulletins; and one morning the excellent Frank Phillips, having overslept, rushed straight from camp bed to studio in night attire just in time to be handed the first few sheets of the bulletin and start reading. As he sat down before the microphone he muttered: 'My God, this chair is cold!' And then he looked down. It had been a warm night and Frank had been sleeping in only the top half of his pyjamas.

Control-room men and the News Room staff were soon crowding to peep through the glass panel at the unique sight of a half-naked newsreader. Men and women fell about with laughter at Phillips – still reading with a beautifully clear diction – with a bare rear end. The bulletin editor took joyous advantage of the situation and kept sending the youngest and most innocent of the news typists into the studio to feed the remaining news pages to Frank. This duty the blushing girl performed with her back turned, handing the pages to him one by one over her shoulder.

I read the News myself one morning because the announcer of the day hadn't turned up in time. I had never spoken on the air before. And that was how I started my career as a broadcaster – by accident. It was presently found that Talbot was a reporter who was able to talk as well as write (the Training School had failed to detect this), and before long, by no means against my will, I was giving news-talks and eye-witness accounts in my own right. I was never *taught* how to speak, never specifically schooled as a commentator. I was at grips with what I really had long wanted to do and I just did it to the best of my powers, learning as I went along and making my mistakes in public. I was lucky to get permission to speak at such a time, when no leisurely run-ups were possible and when the broadcast word had both priority and prime audience.

We were still in the early part of the war, the darkest part, the days of defeats and retreats and every prospect of being invaded and defeated. It was not an auspicious time to become a radio reporter, but I was delighted when the authorities allowed me to be freed altogether from deskbound work and I was appointed an official British war correspondent, uniformed and accountred, accredited to the Allied forces in the field, though still a servant of the BBC. I was a known voice.

Voices were everything in those days, and radio paramount. Newspapers were small; there was no television. It was voices on the air which sustained an anxious and suffering people during the early years of seemingly hopeless reverses. Not just our reporting voices, of course, and not only the tocsin calls of Mr Churchill's addresses to the nation, lusty tonics and life-savers though his famous broadcasts were. Other voices kept our peckers up by making us amused: the comedians'. Maybe at first we laughed in sheer desperation, but it was a vintage, never to be forgotten and never to be repeated radio humour which flourished in that surrounding wartime grimness.

Especially it was 'ITMA – It's That Man Again' which did the trick. Tommy Handley's matchless radio programme of contrived frivolity sprinkled its catch-phrases into everyday conversation. 'Can I do you now, sir?' and It's being so cheerful that keeps me going' were the defiant shouts of blacked-out Britain. We all imitated Jack Train's German spy voice: 'This is Fünf speaking', and it helped us to laugh at the Nazi radio propaganda directed at us every night in the threats of 'Lord Haw-Haw', the traitor William Joyce – by whom, incidentally, I had the distinction of being named as 'one of the chief BBC liars,' in his broadcasts from Hamburg. The 'ITMA' people, Colonel Chinstrap, Ally Oop, Mrs Mopp and all the rest, became national characters, and the Handley programme was essential listening from Wapping to Windsor Castle.

It used to be said that if the war had ended between eight-thirty and nine on a Thursday evening nobody would dare to tell the King until 'ITMA' was over.

The BBC, for its facts and for its fun, had become a mainstay of life in a beleaguered country; and, as a regular broadcaster now, roving the country with an engineer and a microphone, I was part of the National War Effort by words. Sometimes I came into the studios to speak, sometimes I had technical gear stowed into an old limousine, and sometimes we lumbered up and down the country in a monolithic five-ton truck stuffed with cumbersome apparatus for making the heavy twelve-inch discs which were all we had for 'mobile' recording. Speaking 'on the spot' descriptions of wartime scenes and visiting studio centres to contribute 'live inserts' for bulletins and topical programmes, I gradually became one of the household names of broadcasting.

Although, accredited to the armed forces, I was for some time kept in Britain on what was very rightly called the Home Front. I moaned to my masters in Portland Place and to both the Ministry of Information and the War Office, pleading to be sent overseas; but in fact I was incessantly busy in the United Kingdom. I covered the evacuation of the British

Expeditionary Force from the beaches of Dunkirk – a disaster hailed at the time as some sort of victory – the build-up of coastal defences in the South of England and the preparations to resist the German invasion which seemed certain to come; then there was the story of the Battle of Britain, the air attacks on our cities, the furious training of our new armies, coastal forays and commando raids across the Channel.

Then, in 1942, at the time when Tobruk was falling and the Germans seemed set to continue the bad news and conquer North Africa, I was released from domestic chains at last and ordered to the Middle East. Proceed to Cairo and get into the desert war at once, they said.

Which was easier said than done.

3

Correspondent in Khaki

It was the very devil getting into that war. Most frustrating.

The BBC told the War Office how imperative it was to get its correspondent Godfrey Talbot to the desert in Egypt without delay. Weeks of sailing in troopships round the Cape of Good Hope wouldn't do: couldn't I somehow fly direct to the Nile? No, came the Whitehall answer, there was no such thing as flying straight across Europe because the Germans commanded the Continent and a lot of the air above it, and for that matter the enemy dominated the Mediterranean too – that was why the soldiers had to go all the way round Africa and up the Indian Ocean and the Red Sea to get to the Middle East and the war there. The best I could do – and then only after several weeks of trying – was to travel partly by sea and partly by air. The Army Movement Order which eventually reached me as I waited in London sent me to Oban in Scotland to board a merchant ship. A rum way to rush to Cairo!

As a matter of fact, in the Second World War I usually found my journeys to overseas battle stations bizarre and baffling. I reached Egypt that first time, in 1942, only after zigzagging the ocean in Atlantic and West African convoys, narrowly escaping torpedoes, languishing in Lagos, hitch-hiking in civilian aircraft from Nigeria to the Congo and Uganda, and then bucketing down the Nile in a flying-boat. Altogether I was six weeks travelling to Cairo.

Even that trip, however, was no more improbable than the one I made a year later in a strange variety of hard, unpressurized planes, to return to Cairo and beyond after a visit back to London for leave and consultations. Again I had to go far down into Africa – Senegal, the Gambia, the Cameroons and across to Ethiopia – to reach northern Egypt and thence to Sicily and Italy. First I was put aboard an airliner – in civilian clothes, my khaki uniforms packed in my valise – to Portugal and spent a night in Lisbon. That halt was an uncanny experience. To land at an airport blazing with light, to drive into the city in an eager taxi, and to find streets and shops dazzling too, full of plush restaurants and smart people – it was all quite shocking to someone who for four years had been on sombre war fronts and a darkened wartime London where it was hard to get a cab or a decent meal.

I made another war journey through Lisbon at a moment when the Portuguese were in a flap because the news had just broken that they had granted the Allies the use of air bases on the islands of the Azores to protect our shipping in the Atlantic; and they were therefore afraid that the Germans would be so furious at such seeming abandonment of neutrality that they would bomb Lisbon. So everyone was rushing about painting their car headlamps blue and sticking strips of anti-blast brown paper across the windows of their houses. They even turned out one or two of the street lights and broadcast the sound of an air-raid siren over the radio every fifteen minutes so that people would get used to the noise of it. The scene was comical after the experience of the London blitzes. And the Nazi bombers never came.

But the Germans were in Lisbon all right, and the city seemed to be full of them. Technically, Lisbon was a city of peace, but in fact was an international cauldron. Emissaries of every nationality were on furtive business around the place. Lisbon, like Stockholm, that other neutral capital, remained throughout the war an oasis of peacetime normality and a nest of spies and strange encounters. To stay a night there, as I did more than once when travelling to and from the war, was like being given a banquet while half-starved, like finding some Blackpool Illuminations surrounded by utter darkness.

Everything was startling. At the airport on my first landing I gaped at an enemy aircraft right alongside, a Lufthansa plane on civilian shuttle service. I marvelled when fat business-suited Teutons drove nonchalantly off towards the city lights, the well-stocked cafés, the twinkling cinemas, the tarts on the Avenida and the touts in Black Horse Square. I was embarrassed and taken aback on arriving late at night at the Avenida Palace Hotel to be told by an apologetic manager that the dining-room was not working at all and all he could offer was cold supper in my room. The embarrassment was at the riches of the supper: mountains of mutton and chicken, salads, butter, white bread and two bottles of excellent wine. I hadn't seen such a meal for years; and after living either on army rations or a British diet of meatless Woolton pie and burned Spam I could not do justice to the spread.

Stranger still was my hotel meal downstairs next morning. I was given a breakfast of bacon and eggs, croissants, fresh fruit and real coffee – and discovered that the man in the Palm Beach suit with whom I was sharing the table was a German air force officer, in transit and in civvies. He didn't say which way he was going. We made conventional noises, folded our napkins, bowed, and went off to fight each other.

That particular Nazi was smooth enough, but no doubt he was off to some rough enterprise, for his business was to beat the British. Some of his fellows came near to beating me, certainly to ending my career, not many hours afterwards. I got a plane down to Rabat in Morocco and then across to Gibraltar, where I changed into tropical khaki uniform once more. At Gib I contrived to board an old Dakota (was there ever such a ubiquitous workhorse, such an everlasting warhorse, as the DC3?) as part of a load of army officers proceeding in the direction of Algiers and the fronts behind. After a miserable NAAFI lunch, we took off shakily, not made any happier by the knowledge that we were going to fly, in a slow and unarmed machine, through airspace which, if not completely dominated by the enemy, was at any rate a happy hunting ground of some of the Luftwaffe's fighters. As we sat, in two rows facing each other on the hard, tin, backs-to-the wall benches which served as seats in wartime, we presently noticed that our aircraft was flying only a few feet above the waves of the Mediterranean. Then the second pilot came aft and asked us to put on our Mae West lifejackets. This we did, wondering. A few minutes later he appeared again and said would we please get our lap-straps fastened as though for a landing. Seeing that we were miles out over the sea this seemed somewhat peculiar, and one of our number plucked up courage to shout a question to the pilot: 'What's this for, then?' The reply had that studied unconcern which deceives nobody and makes the blood run cold:

'We've spotted a JU88 nosing about. He's crossed our bows a couple of times, and maybe he won't have seen us as we're flying so low. Seems unlikely, though. He's away in the direction of the Spanish coast at the moment. If he comes back and gets on to us, that's it. The skipper says he may have to ditch in the sea. You'd have a bit of time to get out.'

We sat there pretty still, very hot in those jackets. Nobody spoke much. I was frightened, more so than on any of the operational flights I'd been on during the war: we were a sitting duck. We skittered on – and were untouched: the Junkers didn't come back. When eventually we got out of the plane after a slap-bang landing at Maison Blanche airfield, our faces were sweating with more than the heat. One very experienced officer kissed the ground.

I thought of that thankful major when I was impelled to salute a runway myself one day later in the war. I flew with a parachute unit from the Italian front to the fighting in Greece, where British troops, helping to throw out the occupying Germans, were coping with a civil war into the bargain, preventing a takeover by armed bands of partisan Reds. My aircraft was forced down by guerrilla fire on to a makeshift landing strip which would have been rough enough in ordinary circumstance but which was now intermittently cratered and blocked by piles of stones here and there. Nevertheless, our pilot somehow managed to dodge the main obstacles and we jarred to a standstill without overturning. When I tumbled out, with only bruises and a broken recording machine, I myself kissed the ground in thanks and relief.

Eventually I got into liberated Athens – it was at the end of 1944 – to find Constitution Square unconstitutionally perilous, a cesspit of fratricidal strife and a sniper's paradise. The august Hotel Grande Bretagne was British military headquarters, and thus a target for Athenian anarchists. Winston

Churchill arrived there on an icy Christmas Eve, I recall – the Prime Minister had gone to Greece to avert a power snatch by Communists – and soon after he had begun his conferences there, one of our patrols discovered three-quarters of a ton of dynamite ready for exploding under the hotel. 'One of our patrols', as a matter of fact, is the official euphemism which was later used to describe the incident. What happened was that two Scottish soldiers, who had been keeping themselves warm with many drams of the most famous product of their country, decided that they must lever up a drainage inspection cover in the pavement near the hotel's front entrance. This they presently managed to do, and were much affronted to be fired at by persons in the sewer below. The Jocks at once jumped down into the tunnel, saw a party of terrorists making off down one of the passages, and found bundles of explosive, to which the gang had been attaching wires and a detonator. The mine would probably have killed Churchill and the other VIPs, for their talks were going on in a cellar of the hotel. As it was, they escaped thanks to the propensity of warmed-up revellers to indulge in the sport of tipping manhole lids like large tiddly-winks.

Those talks in Athens, in the Grande Bretagne and aboard the cruiser HMS *Ajax* in the Piraeus harbour, were the crisis meetings which resulted in Churchill's approval of an archbishop, the bearded Damaskinos, as Greek Regent to preside over an emergency government assisting the Allied cause and tackling the revolutionary turmoil. Damaskinos, who had been a right-wing resistance leader during the German occupation, was recognized by Winston as the one man who at the time had emerged with moral authority and political sense. The Churchillian phrase said to have described him was: 'This able and ambitious figure, as full of wisdom and craft as a medieval prelate, will suit our purpose.' (An ikon given to him by the Archbishop later had pride of place on a wall of Sir Winston's study at Chartwell).

My own purpose, during my few days in Athens during that wartime year, was to find a way of broadcasting reports out of a chaotic city that was still sporadically a battleground. I did discover a radio transmitter which got my voice across the

Adriatic, to be picked up in Italy and relayed to London. Fortunately, the links were by military wireless and BBC hookups, not commercial channels. So I did not have to pay for my circuits and my air-time. Payment in cash would have been difficult: the currency had collapsed, as I realized when I went into an Athenian bank and asked to change a pound note into local money. I emerged with a kitbag stuffed with notes: the rate was 22,000,000,000,000 drachmas to the pound. . . .

But to return to that first overseas journey of mine, my début as Middle East war correspondent in 1942. There were many problems, but at least no money problems, when at long last I got to Cairo. Piastres were not suffering, except from the contemptuous slang of British troops who called them 'ackers' and threw them around whenever they were out of the line. My principal problem on arriving in the Egyptian capital was getting out of the place and up to the front. The enemy, Rommel and the Afrika Korps, were nearly upon us; they had only just been halted up the desert road at a spot called Alamein; and Cairo was menaced. In England that situation had seemed desperate; I had been sent out rarin' to report the crisis and join the battle.

But now that I was on the spot there seemed to be no atmosphere of danger. It was all anticlimax to me. Cairo, which I had envisaged as a grim outpost tensely awaiting attack from a foe who had so nearly reached the Nile, was madly bright and normal, full of soldiers on leave enjoying the lights. Ezbekia Square, Sharia Kasr el Nil and Fouad el Awal – they were all bristling with busy bars and belly-dance cabarets, and everywhere the Stella beer was flowing freely. The chief memsahibs of the garrison – Lady Lampson and Lady Russell, wives of the Ambassador and the Chief of Police – were absorbed in rivalling each other over sponsoring lush new servicemen's clubs; Shepheard's Hotel and Groppi's cafés were awash with gorgeous khaki playboys who seemed to me to have no connection with the dusty arenas of my new war. I was taken aback.

My colleagues in the sleazy little BBC office in Sharia Gameh Charkass put me in the picture. Their advice was: 'There's no hurry to go up to the desert. Rommel's been stopped at El

Alamein; both sides are digging in up there and a lull is all that's going to happen for some time. The situation is stable and we've got used to it; and anyhow we've got a chap watching out on our behalf with the army. Stop worrying; make your contacts properly here at GHQ before you think of going forward.'

I was sure there was some sense in the advice, but I began to see why my London office had been concerned about lack of first-hand reporting of the desert situation. I had been flattered to be dispatched to this exotic theatre of war; but I now could see the difficulties. We had no one, not even one of our Middle East recording engineers, at the front; and indeed, with almost no action going on in the Alamein box, the temptation to stay in Cairo was considerable – not to me, the new boy, but to the old hands. Even the army Public Relations chiefs counselled me to remain in Cairo for a while.

Everybody in the city appeared unperturbed by the nearness of the enemy and the fact that it was still on the cards that the Axis forces would break through and one day actually enter Cairo. Shopkeepers told me quite openly that they were prepared to be serving German and Italian soldiers next. The King of Egypt himself was wavering. The obese, obscene Farouk (with whom no confidence and no woman was safe: there had been explosive incidents when in night clubs he had begun pawing officers' wives in the presence of their husbands) had come to be regarded as a danger and a doubt in our midst, so much so that he had been threatened in his own palace by the British Ambassador, Sir Miles Lampson; had been ordered to behave and to stop encouraging German sympathizers. Lampson's action was bold and high-handed, no doubt, and it certainly angered a group of young Egyptian army officers led by Gamal Abdel Nasser who, infuriated by this further humiliation inflicted on an enemy-occupied Egypt, secretly swore anew their vows to the nationalism which, in the revolution ten years later, swept out both Farouk and the British. The ambassador's preoccupation was with politics and propaganda rather than the fighting.

I listened to all the stories of the city's intrigues and scandals; I ate comfortable dinners with military press censors at Mena

House and lunches with pashas at the Turf Club; I inspected the Sphinx with sandbags under his chin and was taken shopping in the dark depths of the Khan-al-Khalili bazaar. But I wasn't up in the firing line, and had to accept that for the moment there was scarcely any Middle East war going on.

So it was a bewildered Godfrey Talbot who fretted in hot, noisy Cairo in the summer of 1942. The image I still retain of the city in that period of calm before the storm is not of Rommel at the gate but Richard Dimbleby at the piano.

I had been sent out from London to replace Richard as our Middle East correspondent. He had been recalled to base, accused, not quite fairly, of over-optimism, misreporting, peddling a rosy-hued 'official line' during the retreat; he was in bad odour with both the troops and the BBC in London. It was a strange period in the successful life of broadcasting's best-known reporter – whose years of greatest fame and skilled maturity were still to come.

Dimbleby was our first war correspondent. In 1942 he was experienced and already well known; he had seen a lot of fighting, covered the Middle East disasters which were almost all the war had brought so far. Now he seemed to be enjoying a lull of his own – and the social life of Cairo. If he felt resentment at my arrival to take over, if he was stung by London ordering him home under a cloud, he did not show it. He just seemed to be relaxing hugely in his rather grand way. A stout, authoritative young man in his late twenties, he was an amusing and confident personality, sought after by every party-giver in Gezira and Zamalek. His hilarious stories and talented piano-playing would keep a company going all evening. His talk, like his broadcasts, was full of rolling phrases which came smoothly off the tongue: the smart pronouncements were delivered with such zest that even the clichés seemed brand new. He had a houseboat on the river and he hobnobbed with generals. The Dimbleby panache flourished under the Egyptian sun: he was more rajah than reporter, proud of being 'the BBC' but seeing himself as a roving British diplomat. He rarely consorted with other correspondents.

Richard greeted me briefly but with cordiality. There was little time for professional handing-over because his farewells all round the town and Army GHQ were keeping him busy. There were several postponements of his departure for London. He didn't want to leave. One day, when I was told he had really gone, it turned out that he was only visiting Palestine: he had flown to Jerusalem to collect, of all things, a bottle of Jordan water to take home for a christening (perhaps he had the idea from Sir John Reith, who once sent a man specially to the BBC office in Aberdeen for water from the River Dee to baptize his son in).

Eventually, off he went; and I was in charge. But the war, for the moment, remained maddeningly at a standstill. Anxious to be getting off the mark, I thrashed about for behind-the-scenes stories and desperately sent a series of spoken dispatches, from the Egyptian State Broadcasting studios, describing life in the base areas and such preparations for the coming offensive as the censors would allow me to mention. I was so denied of battle material that I recorded and sent to London – in the middle of African wartime! – a Services' performance of Handel's *Messiah* in the English cathedral on the banks of the Nile. It turned out to be one of the best-remembered broadcasts of that period of the war, and certainly it was one of the strangest *Messiah* occasions I have ever attended. The church was packed with uniformed men and women. From its doors, flung open to the breathless night, the music swelled out over a vast overflow congregation, rows and rows of soldiers and airmen upright on chairs or squatting on the baked ground under a moonlight sky slashed by the moving white fingers of search-lights alert for any raiders who might disturb the sacred songs.

Meanwhile the lull in the desert war continued. I made a trip, via Alexandria, to the Eighth Army's camps and forward areas. The visit confirmed for me the static situation: around the tents and trucks of the entrenched army little was moving save the supply vehicles which came and went ceaselessly, building up strength for the next round, the battle to come. Rommel was held; but so were we. Both sides were arming and reinforcing for the inevitable eruption in the autumn. There was some bombing and strafing, but not much warlike stir on the ground except small nightly sorties from our dug-in positions, adventurous patrols which probed the minefields in the sand and sought information of the enemy's dispositions. That was all. No war. So I returned to Cairo.

Waiting for the fighting to flare was hard to bear. I tried to get into action with the Royal Navy and, hearing that I could get permission to join a convoy to the besieged island of Malta, dashed down to Port Said – only to find that HMS *Manchester*, the cruiser in which I should have taken passage, had just left.

I had missed the boat – luckily, for the ship was sunk on the way.

I heard of another chance. A large submarine, HMS *Porpoise*, was going to try to get through to the island. Off I went to her departure point, Haifa in Palestine, under the shadow of Mount Carmel. This time I was not late and duly boarded the permitted vessel with heavy recording gear and an engineer. We sailed and proceeded westward through the Mediterranean, sometimes on the surface and sometimes beneath it. Down in the stinking-hot control room of the sub we recorded dives and drills, exercises and alarms; and I felt I was getting to grips with risk and reality at last. But when we were little more than a day out a signal was received from naval headquarters in Alexandria: 'BBC personnel must not proceed.' There was no option: we surfaced on a choppy sea and a bouncing boat came alongside and took us off to a Hunt-class destroyer, the *Exmoor*, which was standing by; so in another couple of days I was back on land, disconsolate.

Instead, I ought to have been thankful: the *Porpoise* never made it. I had had another escape.

What was more, I soon discovered that the reason why I had been pulled off the submarine was that things were going to start in the Western Desert. The long lull was about to end and it was time for me to go forward and join the fighting troops at what we used to call 'the sharp end'. So off to Alamein I went at last: Alamein which was just a point on the map, not a town or even a village but merely miles and miles of scrubby yellow plain (even today, when oilfields have been discovered under that camelthorn wilderness where we fought and ran out of petrol, El Alamein is not much of a habitation). And on 23 October the long awaited offensive was started under the direction of a recently arrived general named Bernard

Montgomery, whose victory in the sand has become as large and firm in the history books as Blenheim and Waterloo.

This was the battle I covered as the BBC's Voice in the Desert, living and working in the forward areas of the famous Eighth Army. And for the next year and more my scene of operations, the battlegrounds round which I crawled and ducked, the wide open spaces from which I spoke my dispatches, was the stony desolation of coastal Egypt and Libya and beyond, a hard, scorched region of duststorms and flies, mirages and minefields. A dry, astringent land, healthier than most, for all the dysentery and jaundice. A land in which we seemed to be isolated from the rest of the world; a land inhabited only by the warring armies.

Those armies, as far as I was concerned, were a special breed of oddly dressed soldiers. For there was nothing like the Eighth Army, an arrogant, irreverent race who fought in

'Obviously a this year's model, old man!' was the caption of this forces-newspaper cartoon. The sartorial eccentricities of the Desert Army were immortalized by hundreds of such wartime drawings of The Two Types by Jon – by whose permission this one is reproduced.

tattered shorts and shaggy sheepskins, suède boots and screaming neckscarves. The cartoonist, Jon, immortalized them with
his 'Two Types'. Rats, they called themselves, the Desert Rats,
and indeed many of them lived in holes and looked it: there
was no conventional spit-and-polish about them. But they
were a superb fighting force, fiercely proud of their own ways,
own dress, own slang, own contempt for other armies, own
cunning in the speedy 'brewing up' of either NAAFI tea or
Nazi tanks – and proud also of their own signature tune, 'Lilli
Marlene', itself captured from the Germans.

There was consequently a freemasonry in the Desert Army
to which one was admitted only after its rough experience had
been shared. The real old veterans of the Desert Rats, especially
the men who had been back and forth across the map
with the advances and retreats of Wavell and Auchinleck,
were an exclusive lot. There was even a last touch of chivalry
about their special part of World War Two; and they had
more respect for the Panzergrenadiers opposed to them than
they had for their own laundered base-wallahs back in the
comfortable supply areas of the Delta and the fleshpots of
Cairo.

If an Alamein man is asked – what was it like? – he can only
answer that it was *like* nothing. For you couldn't *see* the
battlefield. So dug-in at the start of the battle were the guns
and tanks and infantry behind the vast fields of sand and stones
where four million mines had been buried, so low were the
profiles of the opposing armies, that all you saw, if sandstorms
allowed, was miles of flatness stretching away to horizons
shimmering under the burning African sun. But once the
offensive started, Alamein was a spitting, thunderous fury;
men and vehicles moved in choking fogs of churned-up yellow
dust rent by the flashes of artillery, the black burst of shells
and the fire of exploding mines. For ten days, before victory
and breakthough came, it was a battle of stand-up frontal
punching, with the infantry and the sappers to the fore, the
guns behind, and the hundreds of tanks waiting to come
through. The Afrika Korps and the Italian divisions on the
one side and our Commonwealth Army on the other, each
force by now immensely strong, tried to batter a hole in the

45

opposing deep defences. The Eighth Army was the attacker: there *had* to be a victory and a turning of the tide of war. But for several days the outcome was uncertain. It was at that time – for flanks could not be turned – a static war: we were hitting at a fortress whose walls were minefields four miles deep. It was entirely different from the previous two years of desert fighting which had consisted of skeleton forces chasing to and fro along the coast of Cyrenaica with armoured cars engaging in cavalry charges and skirmishes hundreds of miles long.

But when General 'Monty' won his fight and got through Rommel's guard, we too started galloping across the landscape, streaming after the retreating columns and fighting into Mersa Matruh, Sidi Barrani, Bardia and Tobruk, past Gazala to the capture of Benghazi, then on to Tripoli and Tunisia beyond. It was an immortal two-thousand-mile march from the gates of Cairo; and Alamein was the springboard of it all.

Alamein was a tremendous campaign to be reporting. Apart from the Russians in the east, it was the only active war front. It was the first victory of the Second World War. So our reports from the desert, by which I was able to send out my own dispatches, the voices of the soldiers and the sounds of battle, held the attention of the world. They were reports laboriously cut by engineers on heavy discs, four minutes on each record, inside our converted thirty-hundredweight army truck called 'Belinda', and sent by dispatch riders to Cairo to be radio-beamed to the BBC in London. Thus there was sometimes a day's time-lag. But it didn't matter: there was a first-class story to tell, and my spoken dispatches were on the air every night, top-of-the-bulletin stuff, heard by millions not only at home in Britain but in the BBC overseas services throughout the world. That was broadcaster's luck.

As our reports from the desert brought the realities of the war into people's homes far away, listeners' letters began to pour in to me from England and from other lands too, written on tiny airgraphs and forwarded to the moving tent of the BBC correspondent by the army post offices of the Middle East. I appreciated those airgraphs even more than the warmest thanks-and-regards cables which began to arrive from my now-satisfied bosses in Portland Place, gratifying though the office telegrams were.

Some of the letters were intensely moving. One from a Tank Corps sergeant's wife, for instance: ' . . . Your voice comes right into the room with us in the Nine o'Clock News and you tell us what our boys are doing, not the old flat communiqué stuff. I sit right up near the set and forget I am in our kitchen in Halifax because when you come on I'm sweating out there with you and it's a lovely link and comfort really so God bless keep you safe.'

I used to get men of the forward troops on the air in my pieces whenever I could. We lugged our cumbersome gear and the heavy old microphone alongside tanks and into gun pits and dugouts and field dressing stations. The Army Commander often heard his soldiers' voices coming back in Radio News Reels in the Overseas Service. Monty listened regularly in his desert caravan, and whenever I came across him he would mention some interview I had done. 'Quite right to let them speak, Talbot,' he would say. 'I don't always approve of what you and the BBC News say, and I've told 'em so in London, but when you get the men talking, that's the thing; it rings true and it's good for morale; keep it up!'

Monty himself received large numbers of letters from soldiers' relatives, and many of them mentioned our broadcasts. Occasionally, when I went to his caravan, he used to show me some of his mail. A surprising number of parents seemed to go to great lengths in describing their sons serving with the Eighth Army – and grumbling about them. They would complain that 'our Jack' or, if it were a wife writing, 'my old man', never wrote letters home and could the General do anything about it? Then there would arrive in my truck a series of notes from the General, handwritten with a broad-nibbed fountain pen. One such note is reproduced overleaf.

A listener's letter which made me a little lumpy in the throat and very conscious of the power of The Wireless was from a mother who had been told that her son, a sapper, had been officially reported 'missing, believed killed' but who, months later, knew without a shadow of a doubt that he was alive. 'I was listening to "the Nine o'Clock"', she wrote, 'when you

47

Godfrey Talbot.
B.B.C. Representative

Ref attached.

Can you arrange for this soldier to be heard by his Father?

I have answered the letter and said you would do it, if possible.

B. L. Montgomery
General.

Eighth Army
27.2.43

came on and you were talking to soldiers left in an Italian hospital which you'd gone to as soon as we captured Benghazi, and suddenly without warning out came my own son's voice saying he was all right. I went down on my knees in front of the set and blessed you.'

Perhaps I was as sentimental as some of my correspondents; but it would be a hard reporter who was not happy to have a letter like that. Reactions from home made the job seem worth while. I enjoyed my desert, even eating sand and sleeping in slit-trenches.

Not that it was exactly fun. Not that the sun always shone; not that that every month brought hot weather: nights are cold in winter in North Africa. When we had advanced over a thousand miles westward from the Nile – and in little more than two months – I spent a miserable Christmas Day in conditions all too 'seasonable'. It was grey and cold and wet. Shorts and tropical shirts had been stuffed away in kitbags; it was thick battledress and jerkins and greatcoats now; and we were shivering under three blankets at night, breaking the ice on a left-out mug of shaving water in the morning. 'We', as usual were a recording engineer, a driver and me. And we were in sorry plight. The truck had broken down and the recording batteries had gone phut; we were out of touch with the army and were stuck in a no-man's-land of desolate and almost trackless plain which we had been navigating by compass; we hadn't much water or food left and were far away from any rations-issuing NAAFI supply dump; we were being sporadically bombed by a German aircraft.

The map said we must be well into Tripolitania, halfway between Agheila and Sirte, probably. We had passed a lonely pillar with one of Mussolini's Fascist eagles on top, and then a little cluster of abandoned dwellings in which Italian colonists had /lived: shoddy, once-white concrete huts with 'Dux' daubed on the walls. I wrote in my diary: 'This is the most miserable situation I have ever been in at Christmas. I feel lost, a failure. I don't know what's happening. I'm getting no news – couldn't send it if I had any. Here, wherever we are, it's – no people, no provender, no warmth, no shelter, not even a fig grove. No water, no snow, not even sand now,

49

because this part of the desert is a tawny nothingness that goes on for ever and ever, covered with a sort of camelthorn bush six inches high, the colour of tobacco ash. If only we had water we could wash and shave decently and cheer ourselves up but I expect if we did find a well there'd be a dead Italian or a mule in it. Pretswell the driver has just made a fire, pouring some of our precious petrol on the ground to do it. He's cooking a stew of bully-beef and ship's biscuits and he's going to boil some sort of biscuit-and-tinned-marmalade pudding which he has wrapped in one of my undervests. This is our Christmas dinner.'

The diary bears witness that I was feeling just a mite sorry for myself. However, later in the day we found some fellow humans. They were a unit of Scots Greys having a rest. Dispersed in a rocky wadi were their tanks and armoured cars – and, to our joy, a workshop truck whose mechanics came and fixed our engine. The Greys' padre held a short open-air Christmas service for his men in the wadi; and we were invited to join the congregation. The padre, a narrow-faced little chap with a broad Glasgow accent, began with the wry dispensation: 'If yon de'il Hitler's airmen take it into their black hearts to come over whilst we're singin' or prayin', ye'll all scatter and no wait for ma amen.'

I mentioned the service later when I was broadcasting again. I had a habit of putting into my pieces some of the lighter and more human moments of the days. They leavened the accounts of battle. And today, looking back over the years, I am not disposed to retail tactics and strategy or the inevitable heavy and harrowing experiences. In any case, the anodyne of time mercifully makes the small and amusing things glow most enduringly in the memory. And I have always found that recollection of certain highly individual *people* brings back very vividly the general flavour of the times.

Thus the uniqueness, the informality, the ordered indiscipline and the rule-breaking triumph of the desert campaign is conjured up in the picture I retain of the eccentric goings-on of a young captain who made himself a one-man publishing group. He was a wild man of Fleet Street named Warwick Charlton. This enthusiastic and unconventional journalist-in-

uniform decided that the troops were lamentably ill-informed
– the only general they'd heard of in the early days was Rommel
– and so, on his own, he started a daily desert newspaper.
Started two of them in fact: *Crusader* and then *Eighth Army
News*. At first he sat in a tent with an old typewriter, hammer-
ing out items he'd heard on BBC broadcasts and paragraphs
hacked out of the army's Intelligence Summaries, duplicating
his typescripts and passing them round as many forward units
of the fighting soldiers he could reach.

Then he stole and repaired one of the military's Mobile
Printing Units abandoned during a retreat, and produced
something which really looked like a newspaper. He sometimes
distributed the paper himself, under fire, delivering copies to
men in shell holes. I once saw him, hatless and tousled, running
crazily alongside a tank in action, throwing a handful of his
news-sheets into the turret whilst guns went off over his head.
He had no fear of fire – or of his superiors, who got very cross
with him indeed: most of the things he did were without
permission and he was always in trouble. In fact his bosses,
the army Public Relations people back at base, hated his guts,
for his habit was to act first and then, and only if he felt like
it, ask for a rubber stamp of approval afterwards.

In the editorials in his papers he was perpetually cocking a
snook at authority. He criticized the General Staff, Monty
himself, Mr Churchill and the Government, the American ally,
and visiting ENSA comedians (for staying too far back). He
voiced the grumbles of the private soldier. He was an ir-
resistible, splendid maverick – and a sheer pain in the neck
to stuffy khaki administrators. Twice put under arrest, once
court-martialled for meddling in politics and for 'conduct
unbecoming', he always emerged unhurt and grinning. His
were the Desert Rats' own papers, and it was his particular
delight to distribute them in a special way: to frontline troops
first, then working backwards deliberately, so that the safer
and more cushy rear area you were in, the later you got your
Eighth Army News. Monty approved of that policy. Surprisingly, General Montgomery liked and defended Charlton.
Sometimes the commander delivered bundles of the outspoken
newspaper himself as he drove about the front. Later, Charlton

and a staff produced a properly printed *Tripoli Times* and, when we had advanced into Europe, pukka army newspapers in Italy. Eventually, though, the Establishment had him sent home.

Because one of the iconoclastic Charlton's pet hates was Middle East Public Relations, whose methods he reckoned begotten by ignorance and propagated by folly, he was scornful of their officer selection. It therefore followed that he had no time for the *Debrett* collection of majors and captains which PR had gathered in the desert to act as conducting officers to war correspondents. My own party was frequently embellished by one or other of these aristocrats and landed gentry as time went on, and I recall a marquis and three baronets, valuable fellow travellers – they had endless supplies of whisky and cigarettes. Really you could not help liking them; nor were they all dolts. One of them, who was with my party for a time – and I am sorry that Charlton, being on leave, missed him, for he might in a curious way have found a fellow spirit – was an original and amusing companion: Captain (later Major, and today Sir Dudley) Forwood of the Scots Guards, former equerry to the Duke of Windsor. He was a young, beautifully polite and upright figure with a shiny pink face, very black hair and a luxuriant upper lip which had never known a razor. He seemed like a courtier out of the eighteenth century, but assumed a manner of behaviour like some character in a P G Wodehouse farce, frivolous and bantering whenever he opened his mouth. It was an act of superb inconsequence on the part of PR to choose the elegant Duddles as conducting officer to a heavy and serious foreigner who came into our midst during the advance: a *Russian* war correspondent, of all things, the first man from the Tass news agency to visit a British front.

Solodovnik had not a great command of English; Dudley spoke no Russian. Solodovnik was an unsmiling ex-colonel of artillery from the Red Army's eastern front; Dudley was a chuckling dilettante who collected wild flowers to press in a book and who pretended that gunfire gave him the vapours. Solodovnik called himself 'narrator of our glorious struggle against the common foe'; whilst Dudley was prone to describe himself as 'glorious nursie of common correspondents'. He would introduce the Soviet fire-eater as 'one of my chicks'. But the ill-assorted pair got on well together after the shocks of first encounter, became firm friends and covered the engagements of the campaign with daring and resource. Captain Forwood's masquerade as a charley cloaked his steel: he was valorous, and nobody's fool. (He is today a revered country baronet in Hampshire, a hunting man, Honorary Director of the Royal Agricultural Society, Official Verderer of the New Forest and Chairman of Cruft's Dog Show.)

Solodovnik I remember as a monumentally earnest fellow, not unlikable on acquaintance. But we did find somewhat tedious his endless questions about tactics, his impatience for battle and his studious pursuit of the English idiom. He walked about with a translation book in his hand, but did not make much headway with it (he and Dudley usually conversed in German, which the uninitiated found startling). He would come up to my truck and ask: 'Tell me, Correspondent Talbot, why can I not find in dictionary the word which is only adjective your soldiers use? It is not perhaps a nice word, I am thinking, but it is most favourite. Yet not among the "ef's" is it contained.'

The Russian was not sure that he approved of the carefree attitudes to the war which the desert soldiers adopted. But one thing he became sure of: his approval of Monty.

This was natural enough. General Bernard Law Montgomery, GOC Eighth Army, was the best known of all the singular characters of the desert. It was not simply because he was the Army Commander; it was because he was a firecracker jumping about all over the place, a spare little figure talking fifty to the dozen, high-pitched and nasal, infectiously confident. His messages to his troops, printed and distributed on handbills before each major attack, were full of playing-field phrases like 'hitting Rommel for six' and Biblical notes urging everyone to pray 'to the Lord Mighty in battle'. Not everybody liked him: many officers in fact loathed his manner and were vociferous partisans of his quieter superior, General Alexander, commanding all Middle East forces. But it had to be admitted that Monty put into that once Rommel-ridden army a spirit never experienced before. His cocky speeches to the soldiers, *at that time*, were worth a whole regiment of men.

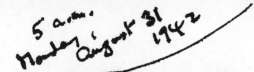

*5 a.m.
Monday August 31
1942*

To Officers and Men of Eighth Army

SPECIAL MESSAGE

1. The enemy is now attempting to break through our positions in order to reach CAIRO, SUEZ, and ALEXANDRIA, and to drive us from EGYPT.

2. The Eighth Army bars the way. It carries a great responsibility, and the whole future of the war will depend on how we carry out our task.

3. We will fight the enemy where we now stand; there will be NO WITHDRAWAL and NO SURRENDER.

Every officer and man must continue to do his duty as long as he has breath in his body.

If each one of us does his duty, we cannot fail; the opportunity will then occur to take the offensive ourselves and to destroy once and for all the enemy forces now in EGYPT.

4. Into battle then, with stout hearts and with the determination to do our duty.

And may God give us the victory.

B. L. Montgomery,
Lieutenant-General.

A typical Montgomery eve-of-battle leaflet – with my annotation at the time. This battle was the last Desert offensive by Rommel, and its defeat paved the way for Monty's victory at Alamein two months later.

I like to think of him best in his earliest desert days, a sharp, foxy man in over-long shorts and knees not yet brown, topped by a sloppy jersey and an Australian bushwhacker's broad-brimmed hat (it was before he adopted the black beret with the two badges on it); an austere and ruthlessly professional New Boss, ferreting through his army's divisions and weeding out the dud officers. 'I've been pretty severe on generals who don't know their stuff and lost men's lives unnecessarily,' he told me one day. It was his own scouring initiative as well as his preponderant strength of guns and infantry and armour which won Alamein.

Monty was still in his fifties, not yet a Field Marshal or a Viscount – and his egotism had not yet swelled into the later ungraciousness which did not easily give credit to others – but clearly a magnificent professional soldier and a rapidly rising star. His knighthood was announced soon after the Desert Victory of 1942 – though there was no opportunity to receive the accolade until we were on the borders of Tunisia in June of the next year and were visited by the King. George the Sixth, looking frail but purposeful, in khaki-drill shorts like the rest of us, tapped Monty on the shoulders as the General knelt down in a tent which his men had decorated incongruously with vine branches and bougainvillaea in an attempt to make it look like an investiture salon.

On the next day the King reviewed the Eighth Army's fine Fourth Indian Division, whose parade appearance was as memorable as its fighting. Many of the Indian soldiers walked barefoot across blistering sand for three miles to the inspection ground, carrying their splendidly polished boots round their necks to make sure that their footwear would be as spotless as their shirts and shorts when the monarch walked before them. The desert 'Sovereign's Parade' did not have quite the snap of Sandhurst but was an extraordinary achievement in the middle of a war, and was as immaculate a sight to report as any of the line-ups I have seen at the Military Academy itself.

I didn't know it at the time, but that North African march-past was the first of my Royal Occasions stretching over thirty years.

4

Peninsular War

George the Sixth's painstaking appearances on battlefields during the Second World War were a measure of that ailing but obdurate man's diligence, sense of duty and fortitude. A simple fact of the times (and not a sycophantic comment) is that he strained himself to share the difficulties and sometimes the dangers of men and women on war service. He was far from robust, not an easy traveller, but he persistently urged Mr Churchill and the Chiefs of Staff to allow him to visit armies in the field. (The journeys were not without risk. Before starting them he had sessions with his personal lawyer to make sure his affairs were in order.)

After we had advanced from Africa into Europe, across the Mediterranean through Sicily and then to the mainland, and were battering a slow way northward up Italy, the King came out from England again and spent ten taxing days with the multi-racial Allied forces deployed from the Adriatic to the Tyrrhenian across that mountainous boot of a country. It was the summer of 1944.

Once he had arrived, he rolled up his sleeves and told the supreme commander, General Alexander (Field Marshal and Earl to be), to see that he went everywhere. So the King bounced about in Royal Navy launches and flew a score of flights up and down the armies' lines in aircraft varying from big four-engined bombers to wispy little artillery spotter planes. Covered in choking white dust from pulverized roads, he jolted for hours under blistering suns as he rode jeeps along diversion tracks through the neglected olive groves of Umbria. Appalled at the devastation, he crunched on foot through the rubble of many front-line towns. He met the soldiers, and he listened – not just to the red-tabbed Staff. He heard opinions from the fighting troops, including veteran infantrymen of a Polish division who not only spat 'To hell with Hitler!' but also told the King that we ought to be fighting the even more accursed Russians, whom they didn't even try to recognize as allies.

There was some ceremonial, of course, for the presenting of decorations. (Sir Oliver Leese was knighted in the field, with shells whistling overhead.) The trouble was that occasionally the war was stopped to stage a parade. One day, when the King's jeep, with the tall dark figure of General Leese at the wheel, was traversing the twisting mountain passes of Tuscany, I saw an army column moving into battle held up for a considerable time because the royal convoy was going to cross its track. The General had not asked for any such delay: some uniformed idiot of an officer had over-reacted to the Protection-of-the-Visitor orders. It was an error typical of the exaggerated commotion which small-time, self-important officials sometimes create over royal visits in peacetime. In embattled Italy it probably cost lives.

Towards the end of one long day the King stood for an hour with gunners in a sandbagged observation post on a ridge north of Arezzo to watch the shelling of the hills where the Germans had their so-called Gothic Line. Then he left to eat an evening meal and sleep the night quietly in a caravan at the army's Tactical Headquarters tucked snugly into a wood in the valley of the Upper Arno. He was the guest of General Leese (who had succeeded Montgomery as Eighth Army Commander) and, though he had asked to be treated as an ordinary visitor, there were men at Army HQ who proudly made the most of the occasion. The General's cook, helped by a few liberated bottles of *chianti* and *lacrima cristi*, had done wonders with army rations (the King said, 'You couldn't get a meal like this in London at any price') and various soldiers had done their bit to see that the Sovereign was comfortable. A certain handyman corporal of the camp staff, having heard well in advance that an Important Person was coming (the advance incognito, fooling nobody, was 'Mr Lion'), spent a week carpentering and polishing a very special wooden seat for the visitor's privy. As soon as the King left, the corporal whipped the seat off the lavatory and later took it home to Birmingham – to hang on his wall as a photograph frame.

As one of the correspondents covering the royal tour, I was presented to His Majesty. He was looking tired (and had often shown his irascibility that week), but evinced interest when my name was said. 'Ah, you're the voice we hear,' he said. 'Now we'll know what you're like – big: the BBC seems to go in in for tall chaps. We listen to you in the News at Windsor. We've wondered how you get through from the front.' I was encouraged to try to explain the business of recording and beaming discs to England. I was able to add that we had now got a semi-mobile transmitter of our own and that BBC engineers had been sent out with it – a great improvement.

We had certainly needed technical expansion for the radio coverage of the war as it was now. By this time, because the Allied armies had mutliplied and, beginning the liberating of the Continent from the south, had spread into the European underbelly, our radio war reporting had grown too. It had to do so. Months before the D-Day landings in Normandy we in the south were deploying a whole network of news broadcasters and technicians in Italy to cover assaults which were far greater and more widespread than North Africa had known. The American Fifth Army was now alongside the celebrated British Eighth in battering against strong German defences. The Italian army had given in; but that made the German task in Italy simpler, and our job no easier. The progress northward was hard and very slow. After the Messina strait crossing it was a case of inching forward up the mainland: Salerno, Naples, Cassino, Pescara, Rome, then on to Florence, Bologna, Ravenna and Milan – those were the mileposts of a bitter and often bogged-down campaign. But to the fighting soldiers it was not the towns but the country and the valleys which spelled the agony; and especially river after bloody river to cross: Volturno, Sangro, Liri, Arno and Po.

In this theatre of war I had been put in charge of a whole team of BBC correspondents and engineers, responsible for the day-to-day load of spoken news. Many able and distinguished colleagues – Wynford Vaughan Thomas and Denis Johnston among them – were now using the old recording truck, for our faithful Belinda had come over to Europe with us and became as well known to the troops in Italy as she had been in North Africa. I have to confess that I always regarded Belinda as really mine, though. She was part of my Alamein which we carried with us, our token of the nostalgia which Desert Army people felt for the old days in the sand. For in this new campaign, cramped by geography, fouled and fogged by the miseries of smashed buildings and civilian refugees, we missed the uncomplicated life and clear-cut issues of the desert war where armies moved fast and free across limitless plains with unity and with understanding. In Italy, although the rough songs we sang were no longer of sand and shuftis but of malaria and mepacrine, we sang them to the old tune of 'Lilli Marlene'.

But there was little time for looking back: I was more than fully occupied. Multiplied though our reporters now were, entrammelled as I was with team organizing, I still contrived to do plenty of broadcasting myself – and still gathered the comebacks too: nice ones when I heard that tank factories in England pinned up placards quoting my dispatches which praised the merits of their products in battle, and nasty ones when some of the troops, having been bombed on a road leading to the front, blamed me for describing on the air the sight of convoys moving along that same highway and, as they alleged, 'giving Jerry ideas'.

Because we were now fighting in a populated land, our broadcasts described a civilian as well as a military scene. And a sad scene it often was. The people of Italy, especially in the south during the first months of the fighting, found themselves exchanging the punishments of Nazi occupation for the privations of a liberation which at first brought destruction and famine. Smashed homes and empty bellies were the founts of a great tide of robbery and banditry, begging and black markets, which surged through Italian life in the wake of the armies' advance.

One day I was driving in a Staff car with an army driver

along the Appian Way across the Pontine marshes between Naples and Rome when we had an accident. It was six-thirty in the morning, soon after dawn, and we were on a straight stretch of road, deserted but wet, not far from Cisterna. Suddenly we went into an inexorable skid, hit a tree, turned over, rolled down a bank and finished in a field. The car landed only slightly bent but very upside-down. The driver and I, dazed but not seriously hurt, were at first trapped inside. When we forced a door open and crawled out, it was to see half a dozen ragged men and boys making off with our baggage and tools from the ripped-open boot of the car. They had thought us dead or knocked-out and were making sure of the loot.

On a road not far away, soon after our accident, an American general was held up in broad daylight and all but kidnapped by an armed band marauding for rations and money. Huge black markets were being organized by Chicago-type gangs. At the same time, numbers of able-bodied rascals were coming forward and offering to fight for the Allies as *partigiani* behind the German lines, killing and harassing the enemy – gangster patriots in fact. (As such they were employed and were useful. It was later, when peace came, that they were troublesome: they had enjoyed being armed and fed in licensed brigandage and were reluctant to become dull, law-abiding citizens overnight.)

Transport was a prime target for stealers in wartime Italy. No vehicle was safe, especially in Naples, which is a vicious city at any time and was in the early 1940s a cesspool of thievery, a city of hillside slums whose teeming dwellings made Fagin's den seem like the Waldorf Astoria. In those days you wouldn't dream of leaving a driveable truck or car unattended for a minute even in daytime in a Neapolitan, or for that matter a Roman street. Everyone carried a heavy padlock and chain so that if he left his vehicle the steering wheel could be tethered to the chassis and then if possible to a lamp-post. It was also a routine precaution to remove the engine's power leads and distributor rotor arm too. Even so, when I had done all those things to my jeep one evening I returned to find it still at the kerbside but resting on its axles because all its wheels had been taken.

But you could feel sorry of the Italians. Naples had been a German-occupied city, and now it was the British and the Americans who were lords. Some of the liberators seemed to be having a very good time too. When the fighting front had moved a little way north, Naples became a leave centre, and entertainment for the troops was quickly organized. ENSA moved smartly into one of the theatres and put on *The Merry Widow* starring Madge Elliott and Cyril Ritchard. But the grandest shows in the city were staged in the beautiful and undamaged San Carlo Opera House; and there it was real Italian opera by Italians which the troops got. To most of the soldiers, sailors and airmen who filled the splendid place for each daily performance, squeezed not only into stalls and balconies but overflowing the two hundred boxes which rise in six tiers to the gilded roof, opera-going, and indeed theatre-going, was a new experience. So they were given some instructions. The British military were the opera sponsors, but the original Italian managing staff had the day-to-day running of the building, and it was they who saw to it that each serviceman and servicewoman who came in could cheaply buy a small pamphlet giving not only the history of the opera house but a set of 'Rules for Spectators', as it was put. The rules were couched in Italianate English. The girls, for instance – the WRNS, the ATS and the WRAAF patrons – were instructed that 'Ladies is not permitted to hold the bonnet or keep the hat'. And for men: 'It is forbid to enter with stick, whip or similar'. Even more oddly, there was: 'No drinking or consummation – and no stabbing'.

I found Rome to be almost as full of rogues as Naples, though the city itself an infinitely pleasanter sight: the retreating German army had left it an 'open town' virtually undamaged. So the crooks of the Eternal City operated in a less tattered and malodorous way, and in a setting of unspoiled grandeur. The spivs and the old Roman socialites too who had crept out of their holes on the departure of the Nazis, now, as the Allies came in, crowded the Borghese Gardens, the Corso and the cafés of the Via Veneto with what seemed to be the old peacetime verve.

Soon the Piazza di Spagna was swirling with American GIs

picking up willing girls, throwing packs of Lucky Strikes and candy bars about, clomping round the fountains in their great boots, their water bottles filled with *vino* flapping against swaying buttocks in tight tropical trousers, as they swaggered up and down in front of historic buildings, asked the way to the Colosseum or sought to visit 'the joint where them guys Keats and Shelley shacked-up'. Uniformed boys with the accents of Hackensack and Oshkosh were avid sightseers on their days-off from 'beating hell out of the goddam Krauts'.

On the day that Rome fell, the BBC party had gone in with the troops; and, within minutes, Belinda and I were in the centre of a sea of cheering people. For months, as our advance neared the capital, the cowed inhabitants, defying German orders which banned radio sets, had listened to our broadcasts on tiny receivers, matchbox crystal sets secreted in kitchens and cellars. They knew our voices. The BBC had brought them undoctored news and undying hope. And now on the day of the Allied entry into the city, they began to say an emotional thank you by bringing out to us their hoarded bottles of wine, their flowers and their embraces. We could hardly disentangle ourselves from the rejoicing crowds in order to get on with our work. The scenes of deliverance were as heartwarming as they were unforgettable.

Less agreeable was the welcome of some of the Roman aristocracy, who surfaced smartly dressed from the drawing rooms and walled gardens of their *palazzos*, discovered the BBC's representative and invited me to a series of immediate and uninhibited snob parties. Those ageing butterflies and beaux, looking like characters from a Wilde play, must have been acting the Vicar of Bray, because for all their frigid sarcasm about the departed Wehrmacht, they had clearly swum with the tides of Fascist and Nazi governments and had not suffered much during the occupation. Lorgnetted *contessas* and high-nosed *principes* fawned upon British officers now, and indeed upon anybody with the liberating armies who seemed to be a name. I was fair game. They prattled happily, and in by no means execrable English, over their glasses of asti spumante. They professed themselves overjoyed at mixing with civilized people again. They appeared to have no cares, except anxiety that their country villas and vineyards in the north should emerge unscathed when the tide of war ebbed from Tuscany too.

And so they talked freely, talked of their time with the Germans: 'Life has been so squalid, my dear, but I will allow that some of the officers were quite well bred. They brought us food if asked to dinner. . . . Well, one had to live! But the *Tedesci* got very jumpy as your advance got nearer. They were ready to run from Rome when the landings at Anzio came behind their lines. Couldn't understand why the Americans didn't press on from the beach-head; there was nothing to stop them.'

I was buttonholed by a tall baron with a luxuriant moustache, who told me he had once been a commentator in the Radio Roma studios under Mussolini and had taken service again when the Germans came – to read out contradictions of my dispatches. He seemed proud of that.

Rome was the scene of some relatively comfortable wartime life for the liberators when the front moved away and the Italian capital became a base for the backroom boys of the army. Groups of our Public Relations Officers, some of whom never saw the war, established themselves in one of the commandeered hotels, the old Albergo Città, now the Hotel de la Ville, in the Via Sistina at the top of the Spanish Steps; and I must say I was grateful enough to the khaki hoteliers of this unit whenever I came back to Rome from the forward areas and wanted a room. Indeed I was usually allocated a top-floor suite with a balcony and a marvellous view across the city to the Vatican and the heights of Monte Mario and the Janiculum. I was also given a pass to go out at night. It was primly worded: 'To Military Police – The bearer is authorized to circulate during the hours of curfew for the purposes of recreation', which meant I could go to the pictures. Or whatever.

Other Roman hotels and office blocks were filled with officers of what was almost a third army in Italy, the Allied Control Commission, swiftly set up to administer the country's newly freed provinces whilst they were still shattered by war. The officers were in considerable numbers and presented a venerable sight. Half the superannuated colonels in retirement in Britain,

it sometimes seemed, had been placed on full pay and whisked
out to the Mediterranean to do a desk job, even if in some
cases their Italian went only a few sentences beyond '*buon
giorno!*'

Two of my war correspondent friends – a brilliant pair,
Christopher Lumby of *The Times* and Cecil Sprigge of the
Guardian – composed a mordant salute to those first heroes of
AMGOT (Allied Military Government of Occupied Terri-
tories). We sang it to the tune of 'Yip Ai-addy Ai-aye', and
the chorus went like this:

> Ancient military gentlemen,
>   Off to govern the world.
> Freed from all their domestic cares,
>   Out of armchairs to run Civil Affairs.
> Cheltenham, Camberley, Cromwell Road
>   Are certain of getting their rents.
> Though they're old and they're bald
>   To the colours they're called,
>   Ancient military gents.

I remember it as one of the funniest press-room ballads of
the war; new and increasingly scandalous verses were composed and atrociously carolled every day. There was bad as
well as good music in Italy.

The particular singing I shall never forget burst out on the
day after the first Allied troops entered Rome. It was a mixture
of hurrahs and hymns. A crowd of many thousands surged
towards St Peter's and packed themselves into the great square,
gazing up at the church, the colonnade and the windows of the
Vatican; and when the Pope came out onto a balcony, a
white-robed figure with arms dramatically uplifted to bless the
multitude, the whole assembly shouted and sang and danced
up and down. There were not only the Christian faithful
present: I saw many newly-emerged partisan fighters of the
Italian underground, Communists stiff with bandoliers and
waving huge red flags.

On the same day, His Holiness – who had been receiving
German soldiers not many days before – gave what must have
been one of the most extraordinary audiences in Vatican history: a reception for British and American war correspondents,

pressmen of all shades and shapes, agency chiefs and news-paper staff writers, together with their photographers, en-gineers and drivers. We were indeed a motley pack. In a lofty chamber lavishly embellished with red silken hangings and huge classic murals, Pius XII stood for an hour in the midst of a sea of noisy news hawks dressed in crumpled and dusty uniforms, a few of the crowd kneeling in reverence and awe but the majority on their feet and jostling to get a good view. When the Pope tried to address the throng, the picture boys surged forward, their cameras whirring and clicking and flashing. Ignoring the horrified hands upraised by attendant clergy and the menacing halberds of plumed and helmeted Swiss Guards, the rude journalistic tide swept on, elbowing and shouting, and the Vicar of Christ was all but knocked to the ground. Every photographer wanted a good picture. They had just come from a field of war and were unaccustomed to the niceties of throne rooms. The sheer clatter of boots on the floor drowned the Pontiff's quavering voice.

One of those present was a little terror, a chunky and com-pletely uninhibited cameraman whose normal stamping-ground was the seamier side of New York. His courage and his crude-ness were legendary; and now, in the heart of the Vatican, he demonstrated that he was as unafraid of cardinals as he was of cops and cannon. For Sammy Goldstein's camera shutter jammed at the crucial moment, and he went berserk. A volley of curses, and his chewing gum, came spluttering out of his mouth as he fumbled fiercely with the camera and, pushing aside an official who was trying to protect the Pope, cried a loud appeal to His Holiness: 'Hold it, Reverend, till I'm in business! Now, one more wave, man. Once again for Sammy!'

It was not an elevating scene, but the Pope managed to maintain an air of smiling calm. At the end of the audience we were lined up and he walked along our ranks, shaking hands as each correspondent was presented, exchanging a few words, giving a blessing and handing out a rosary. He did not speak much, for he was not fluent in English. When my turn came to be presented, he asked: '*Americano?*' No, I said, I was British – BBC from London. At which the Pope raised his eyes to heaven and replied, unfathomably: 'Ah, so beautiful, beautiful!'

Afterwards I went on a tour of that unique sovereign state, the Vatican City, last remnant of the temporal kingdom of bygone popes, a high-walled realm of one hundred enclosed acres, but containing a community complete with its own shops, newspaper, power plant, petrol station, police head-quarters and railway, besides its gardens, palaces and rich apartments. I saw the powerful radio station too, with an-nouncers in cassocks and crucifixes over the microphones.

A strange interlude, that dive into the Vatican. It hardly seemed real when, with the Roman pause over, we got back into the war, back into the hard northward push of the armies which became all the more wearisome because it was slow, all the more disappointing when Alexander's strength in Italy was weakened by the withdrawal from his command of divisions sent to the main assault in north-west Europe and, in August 1944, to a fresh invasion. This time it was landings in southern France; and this time I went in with the invasion bearing some new apparatus, a small box – revolutionary then – in which recordings were made not on disc but on thin wire: yards and yards of it in coils, so that I could talk for many minutes on end. It had been made by US Army radio engineers. Festooned with this new toy, I flew at dawn over the Riviera with a paratroop fleet of tow-planes and gliders, a procession a mile long and at two thousand feet. I lay sweating on my stomach in the nose of our aircraft as we crossed the coast, watching the beautiful and, as it turned out, peaceful shore below, talk-ing into a tiny microphone clipped under my nose and con-nected to the headphones and the box on my back by what felt like a spider's web of cables and switches.

My recordings on wire proved to be technically poor; but the attack they described was totally successful in so far as those landings between Marseilles and Nice were virtually un-opposed; and General Patch's Americans and General de Lattre de Tassigny's French then drove swiftly up the Rhône valley, the French command occasionally plotting a rather devious course to avoid damaging the golden slopes of the great vineyards of the region! These diversions were of some puzzlement to the Frenchmen's transatlantic comrades, the Americans not being a notably wine-worshipping nation.

Now the process of liberation by invasion was spreading and accelerating all over Europe; and after D-Day the broadcast reporting of the war on many fronts became a huge operation. By the time final victory over the Germans was won, dozens of BBC men were in the field, combining many skills, performing a professional job in personal danger. Armed with the virtues of truth and courage – and new technical gear – they forged new broadcasting techniques and securely founded British radio's world reputation for swift, accurate and vivid first-hand news spoken by men on the spot. Our correspondents had become disciplined artists of the crisp word. Outstanding amongst them were Chester Wilmot, Richard Dimbleby, Frank Gillard and Stanley Maxted. Those were the great reporters.

In my own scene of operations – for I came back from France to see the war out in Italy – we reached the end by way of the northern Apenines and the great Emilian plain. The stories we told were of Rimini and Ferrara, Venice and Milan; and when the enemy surrendered we were on the borders of Switzerland and Austria and Yugoslavia.

The final collapse of Germany and the finish of the fighting left most of us with feelings that were not of elation at all. Suddenly we were bereft, limp, with a sense of anticlimax, the numbness of being out of work. Without the din and the dictates of battle, tiredness at last took over.

I remember that on the night of Victory Day in 1945 I had to pull myself together and concentrate hard to satisfy London's request for a summing-up talk on 'impressions of the last months'. And I remember that, as ever, there was more side-lighting than strategy in the dispatch; eccentric cameos crept in. I dwelt on the devastation of lovely Italy, the way bombing and shelling had smashed town after town and yet somehow left standing the features you would expect to be first to topple: the tall brickworks chimneys and the slender campaniles, for instance – and the Leaning Tower.

Pisa was fought-over hotly. For some time we were in the south of the city and the Germans in the north, on the other side of the River Arno. The place became a shambles; much of our southern sector was ruined; and every river bridge was destroyed. When at last we got across and reached the northern parts of Galileo's city there stood the Tower unscratched and reassuringly normal, listing no more than usual. But my jeep driver was astonished and horrified at the sight of it. As we came near, across the rutted turf of the Campo dei Miracoli, I sought to convince him that the structure had been at that improbable angle for eight hundred years and that it would be quite safe to park the jeep beneath it. 'No fear!' he said. 'The bloody thing's going to come down!'

And, with all the shelling, it was a wonder it hadn't.

5

Wringing-out Holland

Back in Britain, peace took an awful lot of getting used to. It was a strange thing of queues and shortages.

The truth was that adjustment to safe civilian life, drab in its strait-jacket of regulations and rationing, was embraced with less than total thankfulness by many of the demobilized men once the euphoria of the first few days with the family was over. The change to civvy street was not unalloyed joy to me, I must confess. I had come back a well-known voice, trailing my small clouds of glory, only to have the clouds scattered for the ephemeral things they were by the chill winds of re-habilitation. A flair for words would not get me any fancy ration book.

But I was fortunate. I was appointed to headquarters and made Chief Reporter of the BBC's News Division, charged with the task of building for the first time a full corps of home-based staff correspondents to cover news and speak their reports and commentaries. The creating of such a force was necessary because when peace came we suddenly had hardly any reporters at all: most of our war correspondents had been recruited either from outside the Corporation or from depart-ments other than News; and now they were returning to teaching, feature writing or sections of administration.

So for me it was good-bye to the old North Region. I settled in London; and at first the organizing job kept my feet firmly under a desk in the Portland Place emporium. But now my itch was for broadcasting, for doing my own reporting at the microphone, not for climbing to some Broadcasting House directorate on a pathway of office memos; and before long

I managed to get a deputy to sit in the chair when I was out of the office. This allowed me on occasional days to get out and about and in front of the mike again.

Before 1945 was over, I covered the long treason trial of the enemy commentator William Joyce at Bow Street, the Old Bailey, the Law Courts and the House of Lords. The trial was a *cause célèbre*, and celebrities flocked to the courts to look and to listen. People slept on London pavements all night to get into the public galleries during the hearings. The nightly snarls of the nasty 'Haw-Haw', insinuating Nazi propaganda over the German wireless, had been widely listened-to in Britain. They were still fresh in wartime memories: 'Jairmany calling! Jairmany calling!' had for years been the familiar nasal opening of radio talks which often gave the impression that Joyce and his masters knew more about what was happening in our own country than the British people at home were allowed to know. And now, although imitations of the man's unmistakable voice were still to be heard as popular mnemonics of the Blitz Days, the ingratiating sneers themselves were no more. Joyce's broadcasting bonanza was over; he was in captivity and on trial for his life. He was charged with being a traitor.

But where was the sinister giant with the words that had the power to make our flesh creep? Where was the monster? Here, in the dock, was only a colourless little chap with no fire in his belly at all. Amazingly still and quiet he was; relaxed, arms folded, but very straight-backed; mild and mumchance every day of the proceedings. Outbursts had been expected, but in the event the voice was simply not heard. He showed no emotion right to the end, certainly no recanting. The doubt and drama of the case was in the man's very impassiveness, in the legal tussles, in British justice bending backwards to be fair, and particularly in the defence's contention that Joyce couldn't be classed a traitor because, though hailing from Britain and holding a British passport, he was American-born, of Irish parentage, and so did not in law hold allegiance to the Sovereign.

After many weeks of trial, conviction, sentence, appeal and appeal dismissal, Lord Haw-Haw was hanged for 'adhering to the King's enemies by broadcasting' – a convinced Nazi to the end.

By the time I came away from the dispassionate final scene I had, if grudgingly, become impressed by the stolid certainty and buttoned-up fanatic dignity which the prisoner displayed – and with the sobering reflection that, if Germany had won the war, the likes of William Joyce would have been stalking our News Room and studios in London, and the likes of Godfrey Talbot might have been in prison or on trial. Or possibly liquidated without any such process of law.

But Germany *didn't* win the war (though she recovered much better than the victors did). *We* won and we were free – free to set about mending, physically certainly and morally if possible, a shattered world. The rebuilding of Europe was a news story which had to be covered by the BBC; and it was some of the coverage which whisked me out of the office and on overseas journeys again.

The biggest rebuilding jobs were on the other side of the Channel and the North Sea. Britain had some bombed cities to repair, but the Continent was left with infinities of ruin; and no nation faced more widespread desolation at the end of the war than the Dutch. Not only was the Netherlands a battle-field; not only were many thousands of her people deported and butchered: the occupying Germans stripped the country of its resources too. They razed the bridges, cratered the roads, wiped out the railway system, removing the rolling stock and even tearing up tracks, so that when the fighting stopped it was the restoration of communications which had to take priority over even the provision of houses. Moreover, the ravages and neglects of war had put Holland in danger of sinking back below the waters of the sea which for centuries had been kept out by herculean walling. In Holland only the dykes hold back the ocean: break a dyke and an overwhelming surge is let in. And in the last year of the war that was precisely what had happened.

The disaster came to one place in particular: Walcheren in Zeeland, the Netherlands province which is nearest to England. Walcheren, an important and well populated island, is almost entirely below sea level and has a history of natural catastrophes by inundation. In modern times, it has suffered from the great storms and floods of February 1953; but it was man-made misfortune which had hit it more terribly seven years earlier, during the war in late 1944. The destruction was inflicted on that part of Holland by her friends: by us, the Allies. We deliberately bombed and breached the island's protecting sea-dykes to flush out the German guns and garrisons there. Walcheren was a heavily defended key-point commanding the Scheldt estuary and the vital approaches to Antwerp, which we desperately needed as a supply port in the final stages of the fighting to liberate North-West Europe. We did get the Germans out of the island – flooded them out. But the invading waters engulfed the Dutch farmers as well as their oppressors.

So in 1945 and '46 the wringing-out of Walcheren, the rescue from drowning of a land we had of necessity spoiled, was – for the British, in recompense, as well as for the Zeelanders – a priority job for the first months of peace. The rescue was an enormous operation; and I went over during a bleak January to cover the last dramatic stages of it. It proved to be the most out-of-the-ordinary and emotive of all my reporting assignments in the recovery years, an exciting experience in which, even as a mere chronicler, I became so involved that the drama of the thing in all its telling details became etched in my mind and has stayed on instant recall.

The first peacetime winter was a hard one. In few places on the Continent could it have felt more raw and chilling than it did on the western seacoast of that Low Countries outpost. Rammekens – that was the place in Walcheren to which I had gone; that was the spot where they were trying to seal the last breach in the dykes. On the map it seemed to be a village a few miles from Flushing, but when I arrived there the impression which struck me was of an awful wasteland. It looked like the world's end as I stood shivering on the mud and from a broken bank stared across the angry, leaden waters of the estuary. I was wearing my old winter-weight battledress (now minus the green and gold 'British War Correspondent' shoulder flashes), three sweaters and a greatcoat, but the ferocious wind seemed to pierce right through me, perhaps because I was at that moment the only still and upright thing on the devastated en. All around, the malevolent tide, black and green, was clawing at the two jaws which were the broken ends of the dyke, sucking at the clay, and trying to carry off the black skeletons of murdered trees just visible above the flood. This was Rammekens Gap, sinister name for a sinister spot.

Much had been done already elsewhere in Walcheren to begin the making of amends for the Royal Air Force's precise bombing which had torn four breaks in the sea walls and let the North Sea in, submerging houses and rich farm fields under lakes of ruinous salt water. The island is like a saucer, eighty square miles big and a dozen miles from rim to rim, with twenty-foot-high dykes round the edge to front the sea; and now three of the four gaps round the saucer had been laboriously sealed in spite of storms which kept sweeping the banks away. Many acres of land had already been pumped clear of water. But the fewer the gaps the more fiercely the great tides roared in and out of the remaining holes. Now there was but one remaining hole, a huge one, and the sea was flinging all its might against it. Here the final and most difficult task faced the thousands of workers: the plugging of the last space, at Rammekens.

A large army of native fighters against their old enemy the sea had been reinforced by British engineers and soldiers and masses of British equipment – generators, pipes, cables, bulldozers, trucks, cranes, tugs, ropes, landing craft, locomotives, huts, rubber boots, timber and sandbags. Mine detectors too, for there were a million German mines beneath the waters. Everything had had to be brought in: Holland herself had been left with nothing but the skill of her water engineers and dyke builders.

Myself, I was gumbooted and leather-jerkined like the rest; and, to be on the spot day and night, I lived for two weeks in a hut with a squad of tireless Dutch dyke experts, solid and splendid people, always full of jokes even in that climate and that miserable place. The weather, once you put your nose outside your hut, wasn't a bit funny – that was my first reaction. Yet after a day or two I ceased to be worried by the cold. I think that was very largely because of my diet, which consisted almost entirely of glasses of strong geneva and bowls of scalding Dutch soup swimming with meat and vegetables. Unfortunately, there was no such central heating for my recording gear. The apparatus which I had taken to Holland in the hope of getting interviews and on-the-spot descriptions kept jamming and freezing-up in the low temperatures. As a result, most of my accounts had to be made by dashing off to a studio in Rotterdam and speaking from there.

The gap at Rammekens had been gradually narrowed to a hundred and fifty feet. But the water in the gap was a full 80 feet deep; and four times a day the tide was ripping through and scouring the channel deeper and deeper. It was a waste of time simply throwing rocks into the deep: they were washed clean away. The pent-up ocean was concentrating on this one point and threatening to break off the challenging ends of the advancing wall. It was quite frightening just to watch the flood charging in and out like a great dark beast.

On D-Day, a day of neap tide chosen for a concerted attempt to seal once and for all this last and most dangerous breach in one final operation, we were all up and out before dawn. Thank heaven, the weather was relatively calm, though still grey and cruelly cold. Snow lay like rock upon the land, and ice on the inland waters. The air froze your nose and your feet. As first light came, we from the huts were tramping across the frozen flats to the place where scores and scores of workmen were moving in Indian file along a low embankment. The men looked like something out of Arctic Alaska. They had thick caps pulled down over ears and forehead, scarves round the neck, jerseys and old coats tied at the waist with cord, British army gas-capes on top, mittens on hands, and big black waterproof boots up to the thighs.

Groups of spectators began to arrive, to view the last battle. People from the towns they were: from Flushing and Middleburg, from Veere and Domburg; people whose houses had been swamped and broken – and still had shellfish on the walls and seaweed up the chimneys. The men and the women were red-nosed and solemn. Some of the women were wearing short topcoats and heavy shawls; and some – perhaps because this was a special day of national struggle against the old watery foe – were in the traditional Zeeland dress of white lace cap, coral necklace, black bodice with a tight waist, black stole, a long billowing skirt and wooden shoes. They looked attractive but underclad.

By mid-morning everything was ready for the fight, the forces of men and machines poised and tense. The day's operation had been planned like a military offensive. We waited for H-Hour, the hour of slack water between ebb and incoming tide: sixty minutes in which everything had to be done. I couldn't help feeling excited; but apprehensive too. I regarded the cheerless day and the horrible sea, shivered anew, but took comfort in what had been done already. The raw stumps of ugly dyke on either side of the hole had been reinforced with heaps of large stones, many hundreds of tons of rock. Woven willow mats had been successfully sunk too, and weighted down with more rock and clay and with black sand which was being pumped day and night through giant pipes from a dredger a mile away. At the end of one of the banks I could see the piece of war wreckage which had been brought into use: smashed and half sunk and firmly embedded in the dyke lay a heavy German barge, once intended for the invasion of England.

But much more was needed to make a giant stopper which would not be swept away from the gap.

Before the moment of action arrived I looked round again at the whole scene. Rammekens even then was an unforgettable sight. Something like two thousand people were now watching from the sides, gazing at the swirling sea and, beside it, the tops of ruined houses and forlorn lines of dead hedges standing out of the water which had overrun their own flat and fertile lands. The dry land immediately in front of us was littered with dingy piles of engineering supplies and mounds of dirt. It reminded me of the slag-heap landscapes of English colliery yards. And in some respects those lines of anxious spectators put me in mind of pit-head crowds I had known at the scenes of colliery disasters. Indeed it was a life-and-death vigil for these Hollanders too. They knew, just as well as the waiting engineers did, that the operation we were about to see would be a risky rescue. Anything might happen. But a last chance of the season now had to be taken: Rammekens *had* to be closed

before the worst winter and spring gales arrived and shattered
even the defences already built.

The hour came. The signal for movement was given by a
hooter. And from that moment all eyes were on one thing: a
vast oblong mass of concrete which lay like a floating block
of flats in the water just off the shore. It was one of the eight-
thousand-ton British-built caissons designed for a 'Mulberry'
artificial harbour which was built on the Normandy invasion
beaches of 1944: a machine of war now serving as an implement
of peace. The plan was that this towering thing should become
the main block across the gap. There it lay, high out of the
water still, with little figures of men walking about on top of
it: engineering staff, directing the operation from the instrument they were using.

The chief of these men – the superintendent, a big Dutchman
whom I had met and been greatly impressed by, a sixty-year-old
with a wide, wise face under a battered slouch hat – gave the
first orders through a megaphone, and the concrete giant began
to move, guided by four steel hawsers which had been run out
from three floating cranes and a couple of bulldozers on land.
Cables tight, the huge thing floated steadily nearer. No flurry.
Very little noise. The sea, the operators, the gallery – all were
calm and almost still. One unforeseen incident came: two
cables became tangled and jammed. The megaphone called for
a push and a pull; and from an attendant armada of little
vessels with steam up, out charged two tugs. In a matter of
seconds they were at the caisson, pushing side by side. The
smoke from their funnels made the sky even blacker. Those
tugmasters moved their ships to an inch, like precision instruments. They shoved, the cables untwisted and steadied,
and in another few minutes the Phoenix was in place in the
entrance to the gap, just as planned. Then it was swung, and
the steel noses at each end buried themselves in the broken
ends of the bank. Immediately, valve wheels at the top of the
caisson were spun, to let water flood inside; and we saw the
whole bulk slowly settle down until its bottom rested on the
uneven bed of the opening far below the waves.

But this was only the beginning. The settling of the hulk
was a sign for furious activity. Tugs and barges and cranes now

came clanking and fussing forward, converging on the caisson from every quarter. As each vessel drew alongside it flung into the water tons of clay and stones, brushwood mattresses and bundles of old torpedo netting. Down into the depths splashed this stuffing, to lodge on the seabed in the gap to fill the spaces below and at the sides of the sunken concrete. We could only hope that it would not all be swept away.

When the tide rose and the thwarted ocean began to lean increasingly against the new barrier, there were still spaces around the gate; and through these the current was streaming. But now there came into play from the seward side a fleet of big steel barges, each with two hundred tons of boulders on board. Each in turn chugged up to the caisson and, when in position, threw out its load. This was spectacularly done. A compartment beneath the barge's waterline being quickly flooded, the whole craft tilted suddenly on its side, periously, and shot its load of stone roaring and splashing into the water, all in a couple of deafening seconds: and then at once the barge righted itself, the crew clinging like monkeys to the rocking rails.

Hour after hour through the day the dumping went on. The tide came up and the water was soon twelve feet higher on the sea side of the new stopgap than on the other side. But that landward side was still a lake of water, and still the tidal rush was coming through interstices in the blockage. Clearly, some holes remained; and as long as they were there the danger remained. They might well be torn into bigger holes. The crowd from the towns stayed on and held its breath.

Night fell. Electric floodlights weirdly lit the scene. The tide turned; the ebb sucked viciously at the still uncertain barrier. Not for a moment did the water demon leave off worrying its latest challenger. Through the hours of darkness, and through the next days, the work of reinforcing the dam continued non-stop. Sandbags, stones, mattresses, more clay, more sand, more slatted mats – thousands of tons of everything were tipped and piled. Anxiety peaked with every tide. When the wind came up, emergency squads stood guard on the banks. At last every little hole seemed plugged and the whole new wall strengthened. But would the dam hold through the winter weeks?

Well, it did. I stayed, and later went back, to see the breach made solid and safe. The Battle of the Gap was won. The water was pumped out from behind the barrier, and Zeeland stood once more behind her ramparts. The people of Walcheren would be able to return to their farms and fields and villages to begin cleansing the houses from slime and the soil from salt: to begin life again.

And that was Rammekens.

Today, thirty years after it happened, as I remember that one little piece of Netherlands history which I tried to describe in the fleeting words of radio commentary, I need very little imagination to hear again the rushing water and feel against my face the eye-watering hostility of the gale coming across those flat polders fronting the grey North Sea. And feel again – romantically, if you like, but the episode does recall the reality of the post-war days we were living in – a sense of satisfaction at a national debt paid, a tingle of triumph at a rescue well done.

I have been to Holland many times since then, usually on plush occasions and living in the warmth and comfort of big hotels, but I never go without a twinge of nostalgia – and of Zeeland-born sciatica too! – that belongs to a gaunt little hut on a grisly dyke so long ago.

6

Wedding at Westminster

There could scarcely have been a greater contrast to my Dutch assignment than the work which engulfed me after I returned from the Netherlands in 1946.

I was ordered by my masters in Broadcasting House to concentrate whatever descriptive powers I had on the *British* scene, and I was given a permanent assistant to look after the Chief Reporter's office so that I could be out doing some reporting myself for much of the time. Among other arrangements, I was appointed the BBC's special correspondent accredited to Buckingham Palace, the first court reporter the Corporation had ever had. The Royal Family was busy; a good deal of news was coming from it and we were anxious to cover this field well. I had not thought of myself for the job, and was surprised and at first uncertain when I heard through the Director-General that consultations between the BBC and the King and his private secretary had produced my name. It was a turning point – but not one that I regret. It was the beginning of my 'Palace beat' which, before I finished pounding it thirty years later, gave me more than a quarter of a million miles of absorbing travel, a lot of hard work but a free ticket to the world, a front seat at great occasions.

Before very long I was coping with a burgeoning royal news story – welcome because it was a story of young love, no less. Life was so drab and difficult in Britain, a depressing struggle against the cuts and controls, that people were more than ready to have their minds drawn to anything cheerful. So when a whiff of romance began to blow through the gossip columns and news bulletins – the dreamlike romance of a king's daughter and a handsome prince – everybody wanted to know the facts. At first there was not much hard news to back the rumours, and the Palace wasn't saying anything; but soon it had to be admitted unofficially that there might be something in the wind.

The story was indeed about Princess Elizabeth, the heir to the throne, and a breezy young naval officer, Prince Philip of Greece, who for all his foreign background was as English as could be in both looks and ways, and was an officer in the British Navy.

From newspaper pictures and the occasional reports, this Philip had been observed to be squiring Her Royal Highness at indoor parties and outside sporting events. Then he was occasionally spotted driving into the Palace – though he used to try to escape notice by going through the tradesmen's entrances at the side. He and the Princess were together whenever possible. Those who saw them had no doubt that they were in love. As a matter of fact, an engagement might have been announced at Christmas, but the King and Queen were about to go on a long tour of South Africa, and they persuaded the couple that no decisions should be taken until after that had been completed. Both Elizabeth and her younger sister, Princess Margaret, were to go with their parents. For the elder daughter, who was twenty years of age, the trip meant four months of 1947 away from Philip. It was a separation she did not relish, nor did he. But they had agreed with the royal parents that the break in their meetings would perhaps be a salutary testing time, an opportunity for them really to know their own minds and be sure of their feelings for one another.

Philip didn't change, and the Princess didn't. She came home from the tour 'quite sure'.

While she was away, the man of her choice had taken British nationality and had become Lieutenant Mountbatten, RN. Very soon, official news of a betrothal was issued. On the night of the announcement, buoyant crowds gathered in front of the Buckingham Palace railings singing 'All the nice girls love a sailor', and they wouldn't go home until the engaged pair came out arm in arm on to the balcony.

The wedding, which took place in November of that year,

War correspondent and Court correspondent

Before taking off in
a Mitchell bomber
for the South of
France invasion,
August 1944

Before retiring from
Palace broadcasting
duties a quarter of a
century later

Above: In 1926, the year of the General Strike which established radio as a universal news medium, chief announcer Stuart Hibberd faces the bulletins and an early microphone

Right, above: Interviewer interviewed – in St Peter's Square, Rome – for a troops' *Messages Home* programme

Left: In 1962, the author, a veteran newsman on special attachment for the BBC's first experiment in local broadcasting, faces a youthful David Dimbleby and a mobile mike

Right, below: Broadcaster presented – at Caserta Palace to King George VI – at the head of a line of war correspondents (page 58)

Wartime Italy, 1944

'There could hardly have been greater contrast in my assignments just after the war. . . .'

From the gaunt gaps in the Dutch sea-walls (pages 72–78) — to the grand gates of Buckingham Palace

Queen Salote of Tonga – here leaving Buckingham Palace for the
Abbey – was the best-loved guest at Queen Elizabeth II's
Coronation in 1953

Six months later the British Queen was the guest of Salote at her
island home in the South Pacific. Walking behind with Prince
Philip is Crown Prince Tungi, now Tonga's king (page 136)

On the equator. As special correspondent aboard the royal ship
Gothic – here with BBC engineer and Navy Signals
assistant – I broadcast the Crossing the Line fun led by
Prince Philip (page 121)

Royal Tour contrasts

Malta 1954. S.S. *Gothic* (left), having carried the Queen round the world, sails past the *Britannia*, also dressed overall, after the new Royal Yacht had taken over as the Sovereign's ship

Berlin 1965. The Queen and Prince Philip, car-borne this time, tour West Germany. They saw that hated barrier, the Berlin Wall at the Potsdamer Platz (page 107)

Down on the farm, with a reluctant lamb; at sea, with a responsive admiral; on West Africa's Gambia river, while recording musicians; doing street interviews in London's West End, with television cameras

brought me, a new and nervous BBC observer of ceremonial, to take post with a microphone at Westminster Abbey for the first of my two decades of state occasion assignments there. In the years that followed, I saw them all, the Coronation of this princess as reigning Queen, the jubilees, the funerals, the star-studded memorial services and national thanksgivings – and the royal weddings. Of those, Princess Elizabeth's own remains best.

It was a winter wedding at an unpropitious time. Nineteen-forty-seven had been a hideous year, even apart from our enduring food and clothing difficulties. We had had months of dreadful frosts, unprecedented floods and prolonged blizzards, all increasing the spartan gloom which an economic crisis and wholesale power cuts had cast upon us. The war had finished two years ago, but coal shortage was crippling industry more drastically than the Luftwaffe's bombs had ever done. No wonder Clement Attlee and his new Labour Government ruled that, royal wedding or not, this was no time for a party. It was stated that there must be no national holiday on the day the Princess got married: everybody should stay at work, even though they were shivering in unheated offices and factories. But governments sometimes have to give way to national sentiment. As the date of the marriage drew near, a great groundswell of public feeling about the wedding began to manifest itself. Surely a bit of jollification for one day would do no harm to the country's trade, and would cheer people's spirits? Pleas for bright colours and joyful noise were taken up by the newspapers and by Members of Parliament; and eventually the Cabinet, who had said that it would have to be an austerity wedding as far as drives through the streets were concerned, bowed to public interest in the affair, had a change of heart and relented enough to allow a few flags, proper escorts for processional carriages, dressed-up soldiery and full military bands. Many people took an unofficial day off anyhow, determined to enjoy whatever was going. And what was going proved splendid, a tonic. Even republicans said so. The wedding shone as a bright light in a dark world.

We were allowed to have microphones and commentators all around the Abbey and along the route of the coaches through the West End streets. Television too, though it was then still a novelty and public officials were nervous of it, was permitted 'live' coverage outside the church, but not within. A few film cameras were allowed in the Abbey – their admitting was reckoned pretty daring by the authorities, and the photographers were restricted in what they could shoot.

As to Sound broadcasting, however, it was a great day; and the wedding received full treatment: the first world hook-up of a new era. Thousands of wireless stations relayed the ceremony, and the whole day was described minute by minute over the air from London in forty-two languages. In France, the electricity cuts which at that time were being imposed daily all over the country were suspended entirely on 20 November so that everybody could tune-in to England. In New York many people got out of bed at six in the morning to sit in front of their parlour radio sets. In China a rash of weddings broke out in Hankow and Shanghai, for Chinese brides thought it lucky to get married on Elizabeth Day.

In London itself, when The Day came, the damp, cold climate was treated contemptuously by the throngs of people in the streets. Many had slept out all the dripping night to get good places at the kerbsides when the pagentry began. For pageant it was, after all. Troops lining the route from Palace to Abbey were in the all-too-familiar khaki, but the men in the processions, the Household Cavalry and the foot soldiers of the Brigade of Guards, appeared in the full-dress and ceremonial uniforms which we had almost forgotten but now were excited to see. One of the big thrills of the occasion was the sight of white and red plumes and burnished breastplates, bearskin caps and scarlet tunics not seen for 8 years. Here they were, deployed before colour-starved eyes, in all their pre-war glory and never a scent of mothballs.

Inside the Abbey the picture was bright too, though it was largely the brightness of the clerical vestments (which in any case are always, in my experience, the most theatrical and gorgeous clothes in the church even when courtiers and congregation are in full fig). There was no mass of gala uniforms, for sober suits and wartime service dress were the rig of the day. That went for the bridegroom too: no ceremonial

attire for him. When Prince Philip slipped into the Abbey, by
way of a little door near Poets' Corner, we saw that he was in
the regulation naval short jacket of a two-ringer, though with
the insignia stars of new royal decorations on the tunic. King
George had made him Duke of Edinburgh the day before – so
the Princess did not have to become Mrs Mountbatten.

My own memories of the wedding are dominated – however
sentimentally old-fashioned and obvious this may sound now –
by the lovely picture the twenty-one-year-old bride made. She
looked a little shy and yet self-possessed as she walked in on
her father's arm, her veil drawn back under a tiara so that you
could see her face, a cool pale girl who that morning had been
sewn into a full-skirted gown of ivory satin with a fitted bodice,
long tight sleeves and a train fifteen feet long. The picture was
sheer Botticelli.

That wedding was fairy-tale stuff, of course. Yet the people
were real. And it was something true and clean and happy,
something steady and good to catch on to – a kind of assurance
that life would get back to normal one day: it was a discernible
step away from bombs and Belsen. Just for the day.

The frank non-austerity of the day was enjoyed. I don't
remember anybody grumbling about the bride's dress, ex-
travagant indulgence though it was. The Princess had been
given a special allowance of a hundred clothing coupons for
the material: the Board of Trade ruled that it was 'a matter of
national prestige'. So twenty-five women in the Hartnell work-
rooms had stitched at the frock for days and days, putting a
hundred thousand little pearls into the embroidery.

In the Abbey two little boys walked behind the bride and
carried the train of the dress. Prince William of Gloucester and
Prince Michael of Kent, five-year-olds in white shirts and tartan
kilts, were so well-drilled and so solemn about their duties
that it was almost a relief when one of them had trouble getting
up the sanctuary steps and got a helping hand from the King.

It was a beautiful service, a treat to hear – as they always are
in the Abbey. A congregation of two thousand savoured the
setting of golden altar and soaring arches, the echoing trumpets
and the streams of panoplied clerics. The bride and groom,
very young, seemed awed in the middle of it all. Those of us

on the spot could hardly hear the Princess's soft 'I will' – but millions throughout the world received the words strong and clear through the radio broadcast.

The congregation was a gathering of Great Ones, and most of them came early. But not all: the church was full and the bride not far away when Winston Churchill arrived; and I remember that the whole assembly rose spontaneously when he came walking slowly in (they didn't stand up when Mr Attlee came, Premier though he was). Mr Churchill caused a stir in the middle of the service too, when he suddenly got up to put on his overcoat against the chill of an unheated Abbey.

The Kings as well as the captains were on parade: besides three generations of our own Royal Family, six kings and six queens attended.

After the ceremony, when the guests were leaving, there was a huddle of royalty outside the Great West Door waiting for their coaches. Numbers of carriages were lined up in the roadway beside Broad Sanctuary; and it was at this stage, I remember, that a small boy in a blue suit was seen wandering round all alone looking at the horses. It seemed as though he had crept out from the front rows of the watching crowd, and a policeman advanced menacingly towards the lad to hoick him back behind the public barriers from which he had apparently escaped. But no, he was an escapee only from the special red carpet. Before the constabulary hand descended on the youngster's neck, a horrified equerry came rushing across from the church door, just beat the policeman to it, and gently led the wanderer back to the VIP ranks in time to bow him into *his* carriage. The boy was King Faisal of Iraq, then aged 12 and a pupil at an English prep school. (He was assassinated in a *coup d'état* in Baghdad 11 years later.)

Few of the sixteen hundred reporters who covered the wedding day saw that incident. Some would undoubtedly have made a meal of it. Visiting commentators had a feast day enough, though, especially when they expatiated wondrously over the spectacle inside the Abbey. The Egyptian radio audience was informed, by an English-speaking broadcaster who noticed the bride's train momentarily bent against a giant candlestick on the sanctuary floor, that 'Her Royal Highness's tail is hooked up on a chandelier'. Listeners beside the Nile must have imagined that a lofting gale was on the rampage through London's most famous church. An American talker had understandable difficulty over the strange things with which the ceremonial guards of royalty are armed on great occasions. Enthusiastically describing the gorgeously dressed Yeomen of the Guard carrying their halberds at their sides, he declared: 'Near to me is one of these special King's Police in his Tudor finery. These men are called Beefburgers, and each one holds a large halibut in his hand.'

The BBC had its fallibilities too. One lovingly remembered bloomer was achieved by our publicity department which, before the wedding, produced for all commentators an admirable dossier of information about the occasion and its participants. On one of its sheets was a biography of the bride, which the careless rapture of a typist had indexed as: 'Full biological details of the Princess'.

Even when the wedding day was over and we were back to the dark of our economic crisis, people sought the afterglow. They queued from seven in the morning, for several days, to enter the Abbey and look at the marriage register and the bouquet of white orchids which the bride, as she was leaving for her honeymoon, sent back to the church to be placed on the tomb of the Unknown Warrior. The fact that you had to stand for up to three hours in the biting cold before you got a foot inside the Abbey door did not daunt the crowds.

As to the wedding presents, five thousand of them, they were put on show for charity in the State Rooms of St James's Palace. For a week or two the display was London's number one tourist attraction, outshining the Crown Jewels in the Tower. Some of the gifts, such as the diamonds from Indian princes, almost looked like the Crown Jewels. However, there was great variety. One doubted whether the home-made kettle-holders would ever be used, but many presents were both utilitarian and desirable. For instance, the inhabitants of Leamington Spa gave a washing machine. Princess Margaret, then seventeen, presented her sister with a picnic basket fully equipped. Many of the contributions from overseas were glittering things, but not Mahatma Gandhi's: he sent a drab piece of lace which he had crocheted himself. There was Maltese embroidery and Irish linen, beaver skins from Hudson's Bay and a lacquer box labelled 'From the Australian Forces in Occupied Japan'. I picked out such things in a broadcast from St James's.

No presents betokened the days in which we were living more than the food parcels and batches of coupons cut from ration books which had been posted to Buckingham Palace from all over the country. Some of these were to be seen on display like all the other presents. I was sorry that it was not possible to put on view in the State Apartments the live turkey which a little girl in Brooklyn, New York City, had caused to be sent to the Princess 'because I know you have so little to eat in England'.

The King went to look at the presents. He marvelled at the riches there, in such poor times. Giving one of his rare smiles, he said: 'A lot of people must have had a lot of nice things stowed away for a very long time.'

Almost exactly twenty-six years after that particular royal wedding I broadcast again from those State Apartments (for television as well this time) and again my work was to describe a display of wedding presents. The occasion was the wedding of the daughter of that Princess Elizabeth, who by the time Princess Anne got married had been reigning Queen for over twenty-one years. Again, Britain was in dire trouble at the time of a royal marriage. The general economic gloom of that 1973, when the country was well advanced in the process of self-garrotting by inflation, strikingly matched the climate of 1947. We therefore had a strangely repeating situation, another sparkling November wedding which gave delight but was an immense incongruity, a flash of cheer when there was little to cheer about. But the Anne–Mark Phillips 'television spectacular' had the biggest audience ever. I was commentating at that one too, with an extraordinary peep behind the scenes.

I will come to that experience in a later chapter.

7

Royalty Rides Again

The bride of 1947 was not able to enjoy carefree life for long. Her father's health was causing anxiety: the strains of war were having their delayed action on a constitution never strong, and the young Princess Elizabeth began to take on more and more of the Sovereign's public duties as soon as the honeymoon was over. A tide was gently ebbing at Buckingham Palace.

Though few but the family knew it, King George's 'cramp in the feet' was dangerous. He was in peril of gangrene and a leg amputation. Typically, he went on with his desk work as diligently as ever and went through as many of his public commitments as he could, though he was in pain and people noticed how drawn his face was. Early in 1949 he was forced to give in and underwent a serious operation, a lumbar sympathectomy. He recovered, but had to resign himself to a quiet life and, as he knew, a precarious one. In 1951 lung cancer was found (it is believed that His Majesty never knew the diagnosis) and this time the surgeons removed a lung. Again, and almost miraculously, a brave spirit helped a frail body to survive, and strength crept slowly back. But there were no more journeys. It was the Princess and her husband who went that autumn on what had been planned as a Sovereign's visit to Canada and the United States – a mammoth tour which the BBC microphone and I covered, speaking reports twice a day for six weeks and travelling ten thousand miles. Every day was packed with engagements, a hustling odyssey which the young couple found exhilarating. But one week of a pace like that would have killed the King. There was worry enough about him even whilst he was living quietly back at home in England.

In fact, on that long journey overseas his daughter carried a sealed envelope. In it was an Accession declaration – the Accession of herself to the throne – and a message to Parliament, to be opened if the King died during the Princess's tour.

The envelope was never opened; and when Her Royal Highness and the Duke of Edinburgh got back to him the King was looking and feeling better. At the 1951 Christmas family gathering he was in good spirits as he discussed with his daughter and son-in-law the next trip which they were to undertake as his representatives, which was a major tour through Australia and New Zealand by way of East Africa. They set out on the visit early in the New Year; but they never reached the Antipodes. They had been gone from Britain less than a week and were making a halfway halt – were in fact four thousand miles away in a Kenyan forest – when George the Sixth died in his sleep at Sandringham.

Elizabeth was Queen at twenty-five.

No quiet life in Buckingham Palace now. Before the new reign was many weeks old, the place was humming like a top. No taking it easy for *this* Sovereign, certainly not for her consort. The Accession of 1952 was the beginning of a new era of widespread activity and quickened pace, of great innovations and enterings into other people's lives such as the British monarchy had never known. Royalty was on the move again, and as never before. With Prince Philip a restless dynamo of enterprise beside her, the new Queen was launched into a heavy programme of public appearances, constitutional duties and visits near and far. She was to become, before many years had passed, the most travelled Head of State in the world.

My job now was to travel when she did. As BBC correspondent reporting on the Royal Family, the fifties and sixties were for me almost perpetual motion. The second Elizabethan Era, animated by a personable young Queen and a quickfire consort, was new-style and was, almost daily, news.

There was so much going on, and so much world interest in the new couple at the head of affairs, that 'the royals' were perpetually in the newspaper headlines and the magazine pictures – to an extent which hardly anybody nowadays realizes or remembers. Today, novelty has gone and kings and queens, far from being placed on pedestals, are given a cool, hard look by newsmen. Royal news items have to fight their way into journalistic output, spoken word or print or picture, in level competition with every other kind of news and indeed under the handicap of a generation of jaundiced sub-editors whose watchword often seems to be 'Cut the royals down to bare bones and, if you have to put them in, put 'em at the bottom of the bulletin.' Whereas there was a rule in the BBC's news department in the early years of the reign that reports concerning the Queen or her relatives, even the merest mention, must always be placed well up. A Radio News Reel edict was that royal items must top the bill no matter what else there was.

That, of course, was overdoing it; and eventually those ordinances were very properly annulled. They were part of what now seems the very prim pattern of those days. It would have been thought absolutely shocking then, for instance, when news of a death or an obituary tribute was broadcast to include a recording of the voice of the dead person. And formality went to absurd lengths: when Tommy Handley died – the world's funniest radio voice, the name a household word – the Corporation's news kulaks made the announcer call him 'Mr Thomas Handley, the comedian.' Some listeners must have wondered if it was indeed Tommy.

But, quirks of news apart, BBC radio had in fact become highly professional and was providing a first-class service. One day it performed a particular service to royalty. Saturday, 26 July 1958, was the day of the ending of the Commonwealth and Empire Games at Cardiff; and the Queen had, weeks before, privately chosen the occasion to announce to the world that she was creating her small son, Charles, the twenty-first Prince of Wales. In the event, Her Majesty made the proclamation without being present: she made it on tape. Just before the Games the Queen's sinus trouble flared up and she had to have a small operation. She couldn't go to Wales. But, as everything had been fixed, by the few people 'in the know', for her to exercise her prerogative concerning the heir's title on this special day in Welsh history and during the year of the Festival of Wales, the Queen turned to the B B C for help. Arrangements were hurriedly made for her to record her voice in her sitting-room at the Palace; and this was done, on the Friday, without anyone but a recording engineer and a liaison officer knowing anything about it. In secrecy, too, the tape was taken down to Cardiff by special messenger under guard.

The result of all this proved to be a most dramatic broadcast, and one which triggered a perfect explosion of Celtic joy at the famous rugby ground, Cardiff Arms Park, that Saturday afternoon. An announcement was made over the loudspeakers saying that Her Majesty had sent a message. Then the Queen's own voice came through, unexpectedly, and the crowd listened in silence. The voice made some predictable remarks about the Games and the Principality's memorable year, and then came this: 'I have decided to mark the year by an act which will I hope give as much pleasure to all Welshmen as it does to me. I intend to create my son, Charles, Prince of Wales today.'

At those words, of which there had been no warning, the whole stadium, already emotionally charged, erupted with a tumult of ear-splitting cheers. Spectators thumped each other on the back and threw hats into the air. The noise went on for two minutes: we had to stop playing the rest of the recording until it had died down, and even when the Queen's voice started again the words were not very audible above the impulsive choruses of 'God Bless the Prince of Wales'. Calm though it was in its delivery, this was the broadcast of the year.

Prince Charles was only nine then – it was eleven years before the next stage of making him Welsh, his Investiture at Caernarvon – and he watched the Cardiff scene and heard his mother's announcement that day by way of a television set in the headmaster's study at Cheam, his preparatory school on the Hampshire–Berkshire border a hundred miles away. His headmaster, who had been let into the secret, was watching the boy, and he said afterwards that Charles looked most embarrassed. When other boys in the room applauded like the Welsh thousands were doing, the shy Prince – for he was a very diffident child in those days – lowered his head and became more red-faced than ever. Years later, when he was being interviewed on the radio, the Prince of Wales said it was at that moment that his 'awful' fate really began to dawn on him 'with the most ghastly inexorable sense'.

The reporting of those Games and the Welsh festival year was for me a small part of a busy 1958. I went to Holland to broadcast the Queen's state visit, I was in Ethiopia and Somaliland with the Duke and Duchess of Gloucester, I covered the World Fair in Brussels and Sir Winston and Lady Churchill's golden wedding which they celebrated on the Riviera, and I had a spell in Paris to report the coming to power of Charles de Gaulle as Premier of France on a wave of Algerian terror and a threat of civil war. But those were short absences: 1958 was a relatively stay-at-home year. During the other years of the fifties and sixties, however, I was abroad for long periods. Royal tours crowded the calendar, and became my main and lawful occasions.

Those tours were endurance tests. One of them lasted a whole 6 months, the first of the Queen's visits to Australia and New Zealand. A dozen other countries were in the same itinerary; we travelled fifty thousand miles and went round the world in the process. Royal tours nowadays have nothing like the length and pace and concentrated programmes of those days. In New Zealand, that time, it was licketysplit week after week for six weeks, a new town every day. Journeying with the official party, broadcasting every day, I experienced some peculiar restrictions and personal difficulties. Every place visited was on holiday: it was always once-in-a-lifetime Royal Visit Day, an official and absolute pause for celebrations. Therefore no one worked, no shop was ever open wherever we were. I could never get laundry done, and it took me a fortnight to buy a toothbrush.

But, hazards of hygiene apart, I enjoyed every safari. The tours were hard work, but given health and stamina, a continual chance-of-a-lifetime. The world was unfolded. I complained, not that there was too much professional sweat and toil, but that there weren't enough hours in the day or eyes in my head to take it all in. Friends have often asked me: 'Didn't you get utterly sick to death of month after month standing on

91

foreign streets doing commentaries on yet another royal progress? Aren't they repetitive puppet shows really? Eternal red carpets and guards of honour and stilted loyal addresses?'

The answer was, and is, that I was often tired but never bored. No two tours were ever the same; none lacked attractive settings. I went to places which tourists pay fortunes to see. And I was lucky in that when I broadcast I didn't have to catalogue the formalities. News agencies gave the facts: I had to supply the colour. That was marvellous, because I could get some of the fun and fallibility into the stories – and there always was something unusual if you looked out for it. I was allowed to relate the off-beat royal moments and also some of the odd broadcasting hoops I had to jump through in sending my dispatches.

Thank goodness things didn't always work out as planned.

There was Sweden in 1956, for instance, one of the early state visits which the Queen and the Duke paid to foreign countries. 'Live' commentary on the arrival in Stockholm by ship had been arranged, and in London the BBC home and overseas programmes were ready and waiting. But as we stood at our outside broadcasting points on the city quayside there was neither sight nor news of the royal yacht, so, after much flap on the telephone to the distant Broadcasting House, schedules were rearranged so that we could 'come up later' whenever the *Britannia* arrived. The Queen's ship, we presently discovered, was still miles away and was having a terrible time. She had been tossed about by storms in the North Sea (*Britannia* has stabilizers but can pitch with the best), had found the Kattegat and the Baltic just as rough, and now, with the wind completely gone, had run into dense fog which brought her speed to a crawl – to the particular annoyance of the Queen's Personal ADC on board, Admiral Earl Mountbatten, Prince Philip's uncle. He had been specially anxious that there should be impeccable timekeeping for the naval ceremonial of the arrival at the landing place in the heart of the capital where his own sister Queen Louise was waiting with her husband, Gustav the Sixth the Swedish monarch, scholarly old bearer of the enchanting title 'King of the Goths and Wends'.

But punctuality was out of the question. The royal yacht

had to fall more and more behind schedule as she groped a hazardous snail's-pace way through the shrouded islands of the Stockholm archipelago – until suddenly the weather cleared and the admiral ordered full speed ahead. And full speed it devastatingly was! *Britannia* left her Swedish and British destroyer escorts behind and came rushing spectacularly along the waterways between the islands like a mad thing. Then the warships, catching up, foamed through narrow passages at twenty knots – when the speed limit was seven. (Government compensation of thousands of pounds had to be paid later to boat and jetty owners whose property was damaged by the wash from tearaway flagship and escorts).

There was relief and jollity when the royal ship did eventually come to the landing place. The pace of everything that happened, including our commentaries, was accelerated by the hour-late arrival, but pageantry was not abandoned. In the excitement of describing all the bedecked flurry, the piping-ashore, the gilded barge, the cuirassed horse-soldiers and the cocked-hatted grandees, I had hardly any time to pay a word of tribute to what struck me as the astonishing punctilio of the *present* King of Sweden, heir to his grandfather's throne. This prince, who is today King Carl the Sixteenth, was ten years old then, but clearly the ceremonial day had made him very conscious of his responsibilities. Bobbing out from behind the tall figure of his grandfather, the small boy, displaying a blue suit and a boundless self-possession, marched solemnly up and down the waiting lines of official welcomers, shaking hands with every general, diplomat and cabinet minster in sight. It was the most professional performance of the day.

My own professional performances in Stockholm later in the day went less smoothly. With half a dozen BBC colleagues, I took part in an elaborately mounted outside broadcast designed to give complete coverage of the royal drive of carriages and cavalry through the city. We had commentators at almost every street corner, and the idea was that as the drive progressed we would hand the descriptive baton over from one microphone point to the next. At no moment would the procession be out of BBC view and hearing. It was a drive to martial music; military bands were strewn along the route, each band ordered to play the national anthems of Britain and Sweden as the royal coach approached. Unfortunately, it turned out that a band had been stationed alongside each point where we had placed a commentator, so every time we 'went over' to our man at whatever point the drive had reached he not only had the royals in his sight but the deafening bands in his – and the listeners' – ears. The broadcast became just national anthems, over and over again. The music drowned any speech, and in any case there was a rule in BBC OBs in those days that a commentator must never talk while a national anthem was being played. Our broadcast must have sounded like a repeating groove of a brass band record. We hardly got a word in. When my turn came I scarcely even tried, but simply gave the cue over to the next chap as soon as my musicians paused for breath. Actually it was very funny; but London didn't think so.

I suffered sabotage even more calamitous when I was commentator one night during the state visit to France which took place in the spring of the following year. From Paris I had to do a 'live insert' into the Nine o'Clock News during a magnificent gala evening at the Opéra, a report spoken from a balcony overlooking the grand staircase just after nine, during the interval. The Queen and Prince Philip duly left their box and went sweeping down in a swirl of jewels and uniforms to take refreshments in the foyer, but, just as I was beginning my piece describing them, a Ruritanian horde of glittering men and women came rushing onto my balcony, clapping and cheering *la reine*, and not only pinned me to the rail but trampled my microphone cable and tore the wire out of its socket. London lost me completely. However, a quick technician linked me up again, shooed the kibitzing crowd back, and told London to try again: they could come over whenever they liked. It was almost at the end of the news bulletin when I heard the announcer say: 'I understand we are receiving Godfrey Talbot now, so – over to him in Paris'.

So once again I started to speak, thinking that this second attempt was at a good moment, for I could see that the Queen was just starting her slow return walk up the steps. Alas, I had not spoken six words before the band of the Garde Républicaine, a few yards from my post, saluted that return by bursting into music. I couldn't speak through the loud sound of it: I just held the microphone – and London, anxious not to lose the link with France again, kept on feeding my Paris output into the radio bulletin. On and on. Just music. Waiting for Talbot.

It was the first and only time that listeners to the Nine o'Clock were treated, as part of a strangely protracted News, to the Grand March from *Aïda*, complete.

That was not, as they say, my night. There had been an earlier disaster too. It was when I had to introduce a 'live' relay of the speeches from the Presidential banquet held at the Elysée Palace. I was positioned with the microphone on a small stage at the side of a room which gave a good view of the top table. I was behind the stage curtains but was easily able to part them so that I had a sufficient gap to peer through and keep an eye on President Coty, who would soon rise to propose the Queen's health. Meanwhile I talked intermittently to our programme people in London on a closed circuit and told them to be ready to cut the music programme and come over to me for a scene-set just before the beginning of the President's remarks and Her Majesty's reply. I would give them a signal.

So there I was, reasonably calm and collected, watching the Heads of State of France and Britain finishing their meal. I was glad that our French contacts had arranged this convenient spot for me. But as the time for talk drew near my content was rudely interrupted by the appearance at my side of one of the Elysée's plain-clothes security men, who wagged a finger at me and firmly closed my peephole, brushing aside my expostulations. I waved passes and credentials papers at him, but it made no difference. He hissed that he knew nothing about my permission to watch, and that if I opened the curtains again he would have to arrest me. Would I please leave at once, he said; for all he knew, I might be an assassin in disguise.

In retrospect, it was pure French farce. But at the time it was a frantic situation. I *had* to see. How else could London be told to switch over? I begged the man to let me stay a little longer and he seemed to agree, though he stayed at my side.

I made one or two surreptitious little tweaks at the curtains and this gave me half-second glimpses of the diners. But the guard spotted my twitchings, and this time he raised his fist, holding the slit in the curtains with his other hand. Now distraught, I began to make a series of open stabs at my gap. Each time I did so the man hit my hand down. Then he put a hand over the microphone which I was holding and started to push me back altogether.

Which is why that particular state banquet broadcast began abruptly, with the voice of the President of France in midsentence. The BBC missed the beginning of the speeches, for they received neither introduction nor any warning from me at all. Broadcasting House in London switched over to Paris of its own accord, having heard Monsieur Coty start. They cursed their man Talbot and wondered what on earth had happened to him and why he didn't speak. But I was by then locked in an undignified struggle with a French policeman, helpless, and the microphone on the floor six metres away.

I should have known that the broadcasting of state banquets from foreign countries is a nightmare for the commentator in charge. As a matter of fact I did know. I had been in trouble at one of these events in Portugal two months before when introducing the speeches of President Craveiro Lopes and my own 'Rainha Isabel' from the Palace in Lisbon. I was one of the guests at the banquet but, as I had to speak 'down the line' several short news reports before the introducing of the direct broadcast of the speeches at the end of the meal, I left my place at table early and spent most of the first part of the evening standing up at the end of the room behind a temporary screen, which was where a microphone had been rigged for me. A squalid position this proved to be. It was beside a door through which food was being carried from the kitchens; it was dark and it was dangerous. Waiter after waiter, charging out from the door bearing delicious loads, trod on my feet, jogged my arm and slopped sauce over the shoulders and lapels of my new tails. By the time the broadcast opened and I spoke the scene-set leading into the Head of State's speech proposing the health of the Queen and the prosperity of Britain, I was in a poor condition: spots of dark brown gravy were on my white shirt front and red wine had soaked one sleeve and both cuffs.

Thus I was not in the best state to cope with the crisis which immediately followed. We had been assured that the President would speak in English – which was why we were broadcasting his words to listeners in Britain without any Portuguese interpreter on hand. But with his opening words came a message to me from an aide at the top table: 'He will talk in Portuguese – throughout.' Panic! We could not inflict six minutes of a foreign tongue upon the Home Service public. Yet he had already started. A colleague thrust into my free hand (the other was grasping a sticky mike) a crumpled sheaf of closely typed papers which bore an English translation of what the President would be saying; and at the same time my friend held the flame of his cigarette lighter over the paper to help me make out the dimly printed words in the gloom behind our screen. We faded out the President, faded up my microphone, and from the English script I stumbled through a reading of the oration, at the same time trying to bend an ear to what General Lopes was saying. This was not easy, especially as I had little command of the Portuguese language. But I struggled on; and after a minute or two a repentant waiter came and held a candle over me (adding blobs of red wax to the rich gravy on my suit), and by this faintly better illumination I rambled uncertainly through the speech, catching a recognizable word from the speaker himself now and then, and thus keeping more or less in step with him. But it was pathetic guesswork, and I finished several sentences ahead. But by then I was past caring, and we let the final stream of Portuguese flow out to England untranslated.

According to the agreed programme, the Queen should have made her speech in reply immediately afterwards but, unaccountably, the toastmaster made no move to announce her. Yet the broadcast had to keep going: I had to 'fill in' with whatever description or background information I could muster. So, keeping an eye on the top table and fumbling through my notes behind that kitchen-door screen, I took up the tale and launched into an unexpected *ad lib*. A long one too: it was six minutes before they summoned the Queen to her feet. By which time my material and my larynx were both exhausted and I was near-delirious in my dreadful corner. The whole evening seemed to have gone wrong. I felt anything could happen. I should not have been surprised if the Sovereign had suddenly spoken in Swahili.

The most traumatic juggling with tongues I had to do was when I 'compèred' a state dinner in Brussels and King Baudouin without warning made a speech which dodged from English to French to Flemish and back to English again. Then there was the terrible time in Copenhagen when the schedule of banquet and speeches, and our own programme, was upset because Her Majesty said she liked the fish and the waiters served her *and everybody else at the banquet* with an unsolicited second helping. It delayed the whole programme, and I had to cut my introduction drastically.

A state dinner in Austria started its speeches so early and so abruptly that I had time only to say: 'This is Schönbrunn Palace –' and off they galloped.

That rather bothered me, I must say, because it was important to describe the scene and explain the setting before the actual speeches were broadcast. Or, rather, I *did* think it important until one incident in America made me have doubts. It happened when the Queen went to New York to address the United Nations at a special General Assembly and the Secretary General, by a colossal mistake, led her to the rostrum a whole half hour ahead of programme. We did just manage to get her microphone switched through to the programmes in London to catch her opening words; and I was told to do a brief scene-set *after* the speech. That seemed to me upside-down and silly, but I obeyed orders. When the listeners' letters came in, it seemed, to my surprise and chagrin, that customers were pleased with the change. Typical of them was the cry of a lady in Worthing: 'How good that for once you put the commentator on when the important part was over! We were able to switch off. It was a welcome difference from what you usually do – make us sit through a dreary warm-up from your chap on the spot before the real thing starts'.

That cut me down to size!

But television was cutting sound broadcasting down to

size, anyhow. From the early fifties onwards I had not only a microphone and a tape recorder with me but usually a film cameraman and his recordist-assistant; and half my job was sending back reels of pictures for television news.

The television crews enjoyed the 'trips with the royals' as much as I did. A young cameraman's assistant rushed up to me one night in a foyer bar of Lisbon's beautiful São Carlos Opera House during another visit to Portugal. His face was flushed and his eyes sparkling. 'Have a drink with me, Godfrey,' he shouted. 'I've met the Queen. She *talked* to me!'

It had not been quite the usual encounter, however. During an interval in the inevitable performance of gala opera, this young enthusiast of ours had been stationed alongside our TV cameraman standing in one of the theatre's corridors along which the royal party was to come. His job was to switch on and hold high at arm's length a powerful electric floodlight so that the photographer could get good pictures of oncoming majesty. The Queen approached, the light shone out brilliantly; but unfortunately our friend, when Her Majesty was only a yard or two away, was so impressed by the sight of the Sovereign and his own proximity that he gave a loyal wave of his arm, causing the light to wobble and his companion to curse. What was more, when the Queen was directly in front of him, he was so carried away by the obeisances of the crowd around him, so gripped by a contagion of courtesy, that he gave a low bow himself, arm and all, with the result that the dazzling spotlight swung down and picked out only the royal feet.

The Queen, accustomed to being the target of lights and lenses, at once found this odd and not at all the way pictures should be taken. She stopped in her tracks and regarded our still-stooping friend. And spoke: 'Why are you shining the light down there instead of up at me?'

At this, our friend came out of his trance and jerked his body erect – and his lighting-arm too, this time playing all the candlepower on the ceiling as he mumbled an apology. Elizabeth the Second smiled, waited until he had got his direction right and herself photographable, then continued on her way.

Well, he *had* met the Queen. Held her up, moreover.

There are often complaints, from the VIPs and the public, about the activities of Press photographers and television cameramen, but these men have a difficult job because they are hedged about by security restrictions. A memorable exception was the glorious free-for-all in Holland in the spring of 1962 when Queen Juliana and Prince Bernhard celebrated their silver wedding and had a hundred and fifty crowned heads and princes as their guests in Amsterdam, including of course Britain's Sovereign and consort. It was a personal party, not a bit starchy. Juliana, democratic and down-to-earth, arranged the programme herself and, for a start, said she would like the camera coverage to be 'as generous as the boys wish'. So at the opening dinner party in a big hotel a horde of photographers gathered early and were addressed by the Netherlands' Queen. She wanted them to get a good picture of all her guests together, and proceeded to line up the cameramen with their tripods in a semicircle in the huge lobby of the hotel. Then she went to the door of the reception room where the guests were sipping a Bols or two before going in to dinner and called them all out into the hall to stand in a group facing the cameras. They were surprised to see a strange object in the centre of the camera brigade: a cuckoo clock on a stand. Queen Juliana had brought it from her country palace of Soestdijk and placed it among the photographers herself, explaining that she wanted it to be a happy photograph but was afraid that when everybody was assembled for the picture they might all look 'as serious as stuck pigs'. She told the photographer next to the clock that there was a trigger he could pull to make the cuckoo work. 'When we're all ready,' she said, 'make the bird pop out and do its noise. They'll all be surprised and will laugh. At that moment, take your pictures'.

A nice idea but the trick wasn't necessary. When the mass of royalty gathered, they were all so relaxed and smiling that the bird was never popped out of its box. The pictures were fine without it.

That was only the start of informality. After dinner Queen Juliana organized everybody into three of Amsterdam's tourist water-buses and sent them chugging round the illuminated canals. There has never been such a tiara-load on the famous waterways. And next morning the Queen chartered four big modern charabancs and took her party to see the bulbfields in the Keukenhof Gardens at Lisse. I think the kings and princesses and archdukes liked the transport even better than the tulips. Most of them had never been in such a thing as a motor coach in their lives; they spent the journeys bobbing in and out of their seats like children, walking up and down the gangways, pressing buttons to make ventilation louvres and windows work, asking questions of the drivers, and marvelling at the built-in cocktail cabinets which these super-charas had – and delightedly flushing the little lavatories at the rear of the coaches.

The Queen of Holland was full of ideas that week, and everything was under her control. At the dinner-dance which she and Prince Bernhard gave, she kept making signs to the Court Chamberlain, who in turn would press a button which sounded a buzzer on the orchestra-stand and regulated the music. Three long buzzes meant they must stop playing, three short ones was the signal to start again, and combinations of longs and shorts were sent for louder and softer, faster and slower.

Holland was certainly 'different' that time. But so too was Belgium when I reported a royal progress there. King Baudouin and Queen Fabiola – from whose wedding in Brussels I had broadcast commenatries two years before – had attended the Dutch party and admired the informal and unpretentious style. They managed to provide Britain's Queen Elizabeth and Prince Philip with a few days free from ceremonial when they visited Belgium, even though it was an official state tour. They left their guests free to tour the battlefields of Flanders by themselves, to see the world's most enormous war cemeteries full of British dead, to go inside the old Cloth Hall at Ypres, once a shattered landmark and now rebuilt, and to stand beside the gigantic Menin Gate memorial where buglers still sound their salute every evening at dusk. And I also remember the Queen, in Poperinghe, climbing a ladder to attend prayers in the little hop-loft chapel of the house where Toc H was born in 1915 in the midst of war.

I stayed on in Belgium after that royal visit to go on a pilgrimage of my own to that other Belgian battlefield, of another era – Waterloo. They didn't take the Queen and Prince Philip there, possibly because they would have received the same shock that most British tourists get when they visit the field of the famous British victory – or at any rate *did* get until recently when the present Duke of Wellington began to put the record straight by erecting some factually informative signposts. Without the efforts of the Duke and his Waterloo Committee, the impression visitors got was that the *French* won the battle. For everything had a Napoleonic slant: the Gallic cock crowing on top of a great monument, the French military eagles galore, the effigies of the Emperor and his marshals, the souvenir shops selling model Chasseurs, the French restaurants, the fried-fish cafés advertising '*chips ioyeux*', the Bonaparte Tavern and the Cinema de la Bataille which endlessly blares a one-sided story of 1815.

You have to look carefully, when you view the waxwork model of the battle which is one of the great attractions of Waterloo, to find British redcoats among the hordes of triumphing French soldiers. But the exhibit as a spectacle is well done, and the building in which it is housed is a fine modern diorama. It is understandable, but it is a pity, that they have called it the 'Naporama'!

Well, the Queen was spared that one! But she has, as a matter of fact, seen worse. One day in Prince Edward Island, Canada, I remember, she was taken on a drive slowly along a shopping street containing a shocker you could hardly miss: a store specializing in religious ornaments that had a very large and garish sign above it – 'The Christorama'. Further along the route was a banner of welcome to the travellers (with the Duke of Edinburgh put first, for once): 'Hi Phil!' it read, and underneath: 'We love you, Liz (and we don't mean Taylor)'!

Who said royal tours were dull?

8

What the Germans Did

Of the many countries royally visited, Canada and the United States have been the most uninhibited and casual in their welcomes. North Americans love to have royalty call on them, but at times they have treated the visitors with sauce and scant ceremony. I once beheld the splendid sight of students on a Montreal university campus playing ring-of-roses round Britain's future Sovereign Lady, chanting 'Rah! Rah! Rah! Betty Windsor! Rah! Rah! Rah!' At a later date I watched the Queen being mercilessly exposed to the lady columnists of the formidable Washington Press Corps at a riotous reception in a large hotel, the gossip writers crowding round their visitor, predatory notebooks to the fore as they fired corncrake-voice questions such as: 'What's Philip like at home?' Reporters at the back, straining to hear the answers, called: 'What was that again, honey?'

The Queen seemed not to dislike the treatment. It was at any rate the antithesis of obsequiousness, which she hates.

This is not to say that Her Majesty and His Royal Highness do not appreciate social graces, good organization, and a degree of formality and good manners. They recognize and relish those things, as connoisseurs of them. So they must have enjoyed going to Germany. Of all the royal visits, nothing has outdone, in style and splendour and sheer variety, the descent of the Queen and her husband upon the Federal Republic in the spring of 1965 – the style of the welcome, that is. It was near to embarrassing. Nothing, not even the most rousing occasions in the United Kingdom and the big countries of the overseas Commonwealth, has ever outdone the fervour of Teuton reception that year. In Bonn, Wiesbaden, Stuttgart, Cologne, Düsseldorf, Hanover and Berlin it was the same: the West Germans, great ones and groundlings alike, flocked to salute and swarm round 'their' Elizabeth and the Herzog von Edinburgh wherever they went, right from the opening night when the organizers literally set the Rhine on fire as a spectacle for the two famous visitors, who were housed in the vast Petersberg Hotel (where Chamberlain had waited upon Hitler in the shameful Munich days) a thousand feet above the river and Bad Godesberg on the other bank.

To many Germans, especially to the older generation, the very fact of a visit by a British monarch, after half a century and two wars, was taken as an act of reconciliation and forgiveness at last, an official dismissing of old antagonisms between the two nations. And the deafening cheers suggested a nostalgia for the days when there was a Leader to *heil*, or perhaps a yearning for bygone monarchy of their own.

The German visit was unmistakably well arranged, not to say over-organized. One of the Ministries in Bonn even issued a booklet telling visiting Press correspondents how to behave, when to queue for their permits and badges, what clothes to wear on what occasion, and how helpful it would be if journalists went about in groups and didn't try to push individual requirements. Any photographer stepping out of line would be arrested. The instructions, needless to say, did not endear the authorities to Fleet Street veterans covering the visit.

It was bows and heel-clicking all the way as far as the Germans were concerned. But regimentation and frustration all the way for the journalists from overseas. I had my own share of trouble, particularly in Bavaria, where sighs for a splendid royal past die hard, but where passes and protocol flourish. And where indeed some people were parting with £100 for a theatre ticket and a chance to be near the Queen at the gala opera.

On the night of that full-dress scintillation in Munich's State Opera House – when even the brilliant scenes of *Rosenkavalier* on the stage were outshone by the spectacle of the glittering audience, itself a hark back – I had to do a running commentary on the arrival in state at the theatre's grand entrance. Good and early, possessed of microphone and every possible identification badge and worker's *laissez-passer*, I stationed myself at the ordained vantage point, which was inside a handsome foyer and at a front first-floor window. This, I had been assured, gave a good sight of the square outside and the entrance steps. But I discovered at once that it did no such thing. It gave a restricted view through a small peephole. It would not do. So I moved five paces along to a bigger and better window – I had the whole vast foyer to myself so there was no problem. But wasn't there! Two figures swiftly materialized at my side, two men in evening clothes as I was. They bowed and clicked and announced that they were there to help me.

'Fine,' I said. 'Let's get this window opened for a start: then I'll have an even better view and the outside sound will come through nicely.' The pair, however, shook their heads at this, and revealed themselves as police detectives (shades of the Elysée!), and asked to see my ticket and permit for the evening. On inspecting these, they declared that I must return to the original tiny window. When I protested and asked why – who was going to be at the big window? – they said nobody, for the whole gallery was for me, the BBC man.

'Then why, in heaven's name . . . ?' I began, but I was interrupted by a pitying smile and admonitory finger from the elder of my two 'helpers'. My heart sank as he told me (and it was not the first time on this trip that I had heard the words), 'It is not permitted to move'. The ticket said that my broadcasting point was the *small* window – and that was enough for a German mind. Whatever the simplest common sense might dictate, the small window it had to be.

'Kindly not to depart from here, Herr Talbot,' quoth the officer. 'We have no authority to move you.'

The situation was idiotic of course, unbelievable but tiresomely true. I was up against an all-too-familiar inflexibility. Happily, when the floodlights came up on the square outside, the crowd now numbering scores of thousands began to cheer, and the procession of cavalry and carriages clattered into view, the law-enforcement pair were overcome by their own passions to see the *Königin* and *Herzog*. Having moved from my side, they themselves were peering through an excellent window at the far end of the foyer. So I quietly went to my bigger peep-hole after all, managed to force the casement open to lean out and get all the sound effects, and made my commentary. But before I had finished, the policemen noticed me, ran towards me waving in protest, and shut the window with a bang. I cursed them for spoiling my piece, but they only smiled and clicked maddeningly. Afterwards, the best they could do in the way of an apology was to say: 'We must be correct and do our duty. We regret that the British are not obedient to orders.'

To which I added: 'However silly.'

It was a jarring note in an evening of festive international *versöhnung*. But I soon got over it. The incident was the only sad one in the two days of sheer joy which I experienced in Munich (I guess the policemen were Prussians, not Bavarians at all). The warm-hearted city was in a state of carnival bon-homie and all togged up. People danced in the streets and beer flowed as though it was a *pfennig* a pint. Everybody who possessed traditional clothes wore them while the Queen was around. You could hardly move for men in short leather pants and half socks and little green pork-pie hats with shaving brushes stuck in them. And when I went into the Radio München building and found the studio which had been allocated to the visiting BBC for royal visit transmissions, behold, the technical assistant at our control panel was an ample, smiling *frau* who had decked herself for the day in the full glory of dazzling and voluminous Alpine dirndl. Un-impeded by the fancy dress, she not only turned the knobs and flicked the switches with confidence and dexterity, but kept sweeping in and out of the studio to organize the filling of two-pint beer mugs with which we had been kindly furnished.

It seemed to be the most natural thing in the world to bid our technician *auf wiedersehen* with a smacking great kiss.

The German rejoicing went on day after day and – after the Queen and Duke had taken a week-end pause for breath at Schloss Salem, the home of the Margravine of Baden, Prince Philip's sister – it reached a crescendo when the travellers flew over the Iron Curtain and, on Ascension Day, descended on the divided city of Berlin and, during a six-hour stay, took the place by storm. Dense crowds of chanting, flag-waving people jammed the square in West Berlin which is now called John F. Kennedy Platz and saw the Queen appear before them in front of the Schoneberg Rathaus and sign her name in the city's Golden Book. She then made a speech, telling Mayor Willy Brandt and everybody else about her own German ancestry, pledging British friendship and support for the city, and calling her visit 'unforgettable'.

Her tour was in West Berlin only, but there was a brief, sobering view of the Russian-dominated East too when, during a long afternoon drive through the streets of the West in an open car, the Queen and her husband saw the hated Wall – saw it twice, at the Potsdamer Platz and at the Brandenburg Gate. The *platz*, once the bustling centre of Berlin, was a desert of concrete and steel, the Gate a grim skeleton with the obscene slash of ugly grey brick and barbed wire stretched in front of it: the Berlin Wall, which had bisected the city since 1961, barrier between the worlds of East and West. It was an evil sight.

The Queen's car slowed and momentarily stopped twenty yards from the face of the Gate, and a frowning Brandt and Chancellor Erhard, who were riding with the visitors, explained the history and course of the tragic border confronting them. Prince Philip stood up in the car and took photographs, pointed to the ruined Unter den Linden and the armed sentries on the other side, got a glimpse of a couple of hundred craning, silent East Berliners being shooed away from the border by Communist police, and waved cheerfully to four slouching and ill-uniformed East German guards raking him with binoculars from a platform on the other side of the line. (One guard actually waved back and beckoned. He was probably disciplined that night).

But the Queen, sitting still and looking very serious, glanced only for a matter of seconds at the Wall, then deliberately turned her head away and kept her face averted from it until presently the car drove away, back to the West, back to the gaiety and the cheers. 'I wonder,' said a German commentator who was watching the scene with me, 'if she was considering what it would be like if this rampart of inhumanity had been driven through the middle of Piccadilly.'

Next day, the great city and port of Hamburg gave a greeting as pleased and wild as Berlin's. Hamburg was the place of the travellers' last day of the tour, and of our final commentaries. It brought something of a broadcasting sensation – from Richard Dimbleby. My famous colleague – who seemed as full of vigour as ever but in fact was in the last few months of an all-too-short life, secretly fighting cancer – had become television's principal and expected voice on occasions of state; he was a pillar of broadcasting, almost a national institution, fluent and correct and unflappable. On the Hamburg departure night my microphone-reporting point was near his camera-reporting cubicle, in which he was extremely busy, for BBC television was carrying extensive coverage of the final German scenes. Richard was in full song, hot and a bit harassed but doing a first-class job as usual when suddenly the lines to London broke, the Eurovision link faltered and transmission was cut. An engineer waved a 'wash-out' hand signal and told Richard it was no use going on, for the BBC wasn't receiving anything. So, with no more than a sigh and a groan, he stopped speaking. It was one of those infuriating moments which commentators get, which they try to be patient about, but which always make them cross. However, the innate philosophy and professional discipline which he possessed managed to keep the Dimbleby annoyance bottled up.

And the break that time was very short. Communications with London, sound and vision, were soon restored and the broadcast of the final German scenes went on. Richard, much relieved that all the effort being put in was not lost, resumed his description with words grandiloquently matching the pictures of Hamburg *en fête*. But the gremlins had not finished. An apologetic message again came that the link had broken, that the public weren't hearing anything. 'London not getting us' was again the message scribbled to the commentator. This time it was too much. Richard Dimbley flung down his notes, banged his hand dispairingly on his forehead, and uttered an exasperated cry: 'Jesus wept!'

But he had *not* been cut off. The message about a second breakdown was a misunderstanding and a false alarm. Dimbleby had been still very much 'on the air' and the involuntary oath which had burst out of him was heard by the world, loud and clear.

It was the most famous lapse since Tommy Woodrooffe in 1937 – and its audience was infinitely greater than the one which had heard 'the Fleet's lit up'. The London newspapers next morning had a feast over the accident. Dimbleby was in the front page headlines and his slip was the delighted talking point of a million breakfast tables. The general reaction was 'What fun!' and 'Thank God the man is human!' The exclamation was reckoned the hit of the Hamburg evening.

For us in Hamburg, however, the shout was not the most embarrassing moment of our tour finale. The evening produced some different distress. My closing assignment was a description of the actual departure of the visitors, and for this broadcast a microphone point had been fixed for me on the harbourside overlooking the royal yacht *Britannia*, which now had the Queen and Prince Philip on board and was ready to take them away to England at the conclusion of the German tour. The tour's last moments produced the only real hitch.

Alongside the Queen's yacht lay two British frigates which would escort her home, HMS *Lowestoft* and HMS *Blackpool*, and two big German destroyers, the *Hamburg* and the *Schleswig-Holstein*. All five ships were dressed overall, and therefore there had to be the drill of undressing at the end of the day. All the strings of flags on all those vessels were to be hauled down together, smartly and ceremonially of course. But when, as a preliminary to the royal departure, the signal was given for this piece of theatre, the act was not, alas, a simultaneous one. The halyards on the *Britannia* were pulled away in a matter of seconds, silently and with great efficiency, so that the lines of bright signals above the masts fell and vanished almost as if by magic. The two ships of the Royal Navy also carried out the drill expeditiously. So did one of the German warships, as smartly and swiftly as any *Kapitän-Admiral* could have wished. But not the fifth vessel.

Things went hideously wrong aboard that destroyer of the Federal Navy. Her ropes of bright bunting sagged but did not come away: the flags lay tangled upon rails and upperworks, caught on some snag and twisted in handling. I was giving a commentary at the time, and in all sympathy tried not to concentrate on the agony of frenzied men on that luckless deck. But, unhappily, all the world had to watch, and to wait for this ship to complete the manoeuvre. As German sailors ran up and down, tearing frantically at their lines, everybody's eyes were on them – the royal couple on *Britannia*'s floodlit poop, the ship's companies of the four other ships standing to attention, and the thousands of spectators thick on the water-sides. The ship's officers shouted and blew whistles, more sailors were waved forward to help, and the band on the un-fortunate vessels' quarterdeck played its prearranged tune over and over again as the tangle of ropes was pulled and hacked. The ceremony of departure could not take place until that last vessel was ready. We looked; we waited; we prayed for the poor, sweating seamen. It was all very disconcerting.

Only after what seemed a long hiatus of desperate struggling was the mess cleared and the signal given for the anthems, the salutes, the farewell songs, the fireworks, the sirens and the cheers of the Last Farewell. With the whole harbour a pande-monium of colour and noise, the royal yacht began to edge away from the quay and out into the Elbe on a tide of happy excitement.

Joy was unconfined – except aboard one sorrowing warship where seamen's hands were bleeding and the wardroom's air blue with the curses of a poor Lieutenant of Flags, whose oaths no doubt would have made the earlier lamentations of Mr Dimbleby insipid by comparison. But at least he wasn't heard by millions.

As I went back into the city from the harbour – I still had to speak a 'midnight roundup' to our News Room in London – and made for the hospitable studio microphone in the Nord-deutscher Rundfunk building, I thought what a suitable night this would be to hang up on the Hamburg studio door a notice I had once seen in another broadcasting place during my commentator's wanderings. It was, I remembered, over the entrance to a far-from-grand radio studio in distant Guyana, and it dwarfed the usual perfunctory 'No Smoking' notice. This particular warning was in large letters:

'NO INDECENT LANGUAGE!'

9

'Hello London!'

Studios abroad were surprise after surprise.

To get my stories back to London from various parts of the world, to make recordings to be beamed to my employers in Portland Place, I broadcast from some very odd spots indeed. Sometimes it wasn't from a studio at all. Sometimes it was the cramped balcony of a hotel bedroom, or a telephone box or a temple, the roof of a factory, the top of a crane, the bow of a canoe. Several times it has been from a certain attic in Windsor Castle which commands a view of both the banqueting hall inside and the quadrangle of state arrivals outside.

I have talked into an assortment of microphones too – things like big pepper pots, knobkerries and cudgels; mikes embedded in chunks of marble, mikes like cages which you had to put to your lips; mikes you clipped to your throat; and tiny sensitive bits of metal worn unobtrusively on a lapel or snapped onto a necktie.

Such were the spots, such the devices, out of which I was ever hopefully calling BBC traffic managers far away, and thence, when the short-wave circuits were kind, the listeners.

I remember the stories by their points of utterance, the strange surroundings from which I often had to speak.

It was 'Hello London!' one tropical evening from a palm-leaf hut in the bush outside Lagos in the days before Nigeria became bureaucratic, militarized and strife-ridden. The hut was a radio station from which I was supposed to be speaking a report on a conference in Lagos. Its microphone was a box-like affair suspended by string from the roof, and I sat before it, script in hand, gazing through a window open to the

chirpings of the African night, whilst two charmingly polite
local engineers took turns at another mike and tried to raise
London for me. The technicians were very black and shining
and smiling. Their happy twiddling of the control knobs in
front of them was unimpeded by the flowing sleeves of their
long white robes. London wasn't answering, but they patiently
went on with their calling: 'Is anybody listening? Can you hear,
good BBC? It is Lagos who calls. Please send a message if you
will, for it is only that we have your Mister Godfrey here.'

When eventually they had got me through, I stayed to hear
one of the engineers turn news-reader and speak a short bulletin
for their local programme, which used to broadcast in cal-
culated pidgin-English. I listened enchanted as the speaker
dismissed my conference, for his African audience, as 'big
palaver, dis, and much humbug'. Of the rather splendid
official lunch for the convention delegates he said: 'Cook done
make all ting – plenty beef, plenty cassava, plenty mango,
plenty kinda bird, plenty fine chop and palm wine, all good for
dose fellas bellies.'

He might well have been the African who years later uttered
the celebrated description of the Duke of Edinburgh: 'Number
One Fella belong Missis Queen.' What I do know is that after
two or three Lagos nights like this I became infected by the
jargon and found myself larding my conversation with pidgin
and with the deep 'A-ha!' which in West Africa has so many
nuances that it can mean anything from 'I told you so' to
'How's your grandmother?'

Broadcasting to England from distant hot countries had its
technical problems. Sunspots caused complete fade-outs, and
tropical storms brought crackling interference and poor reception. There were personal difficulties too. Engineers more
than once came on the line saying: 'Will you ask Mr Talbot
to stop tapping on the microphone whilst he's speaking? Or is
it that he keeps drumming the table with a finger?' Actually
it wasn't either: it was drips of perspiration falling on the
mike from the end of my nose.

Hot and stickly weather was something I found specially
trying in Central and South America. It was not easy to preserve
the image of the BBC representative as a decently dressed man

when working hard in temperatures of ninety-eight in the shade and humidity like that of a Turkish bath. At a Brazilian party I once heard a cool and elegant beauty-parloured creature say, as she understandably wrinkled her nose: 'Is that man in the crumpled suit really Godfrey Talbot?' I could have told her that however sorry and sodden my suit was, I was in even worse case underneath, where my fifth clean shirt of the day was already a wet rag.

Perhaps I should have been glad that she got my name right. At some of the remoter radio stations I have been announced as Señor Talipot, Sir Jeffrey Tallboy, Dr Godofredo, Mr Turbot and, once in Shiraz, Mohammed Tablet. Not that I could complain. My own botching of names, especially in Latin America, was probably much worse. I did not find it easy to ask the way to the studio of the 'Associcão Brasileira de Radio e Televisão.' Nor did it come naturally to me, when I I was in an up-country station, limp and squirming on a bug-infested cane chair, to remember to call Rio de Janeiro correctly and recognizably. For 'Hello Rio' was no good: it had to be 'Ola! Ola Heeoh!'

One thing all the foreign studios had in common was courteous helpfulness. They were almost always very intrigued by a BBC visit; and were hospitable, going to great lengths to make me comfortable as far as conditions permitted. In Georgetown, Guyana, a gay little wooden city beside the Demerara River, they brought the director's favourite arm-chair for me to sit in whilst I called up London, and placed a long cold glass of rum punch beside the microphone. Clearly, drinking was not forbidden in the studio, even if smoking and spitting and bad language were. They seemed, in fact, to be a good, God-fearing people, addicted to the battle-cries of the gospel hall. I used to approach the radio building under a banner which stretched across a road and bade me 'Prepare to Meet thy Maker'.

Georgetown specialized in eccentricities, not to mention the dog-sized rat which kept appearing in my bedroom. There were other pests in the town when I was there, human ones who had started a choke-and-rob epidemic. This was a simple form of banditry. The thieves walked about in pairs and crept up behind the selected victim. One man would put a throttling arm round the prey's neck while his companion rifled pockets. The robbers had become so daring that I was warned by my hotel that it was dangerous to walk down the road alone even in the early part of the evening, for I might well be mugged. I was, however, assured that the menace ought to be over in a few days' time because the government had sent for a Scotland Yard expert to show them how to tackle it and what the local police should do.

The British policeman did come – and, on arrival from the airport, was choked and robbed on the steps of the hotel.

But, in spite of this and many other sorts of trouble which they have, the Guyanans are a cheerful people. Their joy in festive occasions and their public demonstrations of simple happiness is characteristic of the African and Asian countries from which most of their ancestors came. When the Queen went to Guyana – which was in its last year of being British Guiana – everybody had a marvellous junket. The only upsetting things which I remember from that week were a bomb scare on the railway and a bad deed by a monkey, which stole the West Indies Archbishop's CMG decoration from His Grace's bedroom whilst Dr Knight was preparing to dress for the official welcoming party.

When the royal party arrived and drove in procession through the crowded streets of the town, I had a place in one of the cars of the procession. With a tape recorder in my lap and a helpful government information officer beside me, I made a commentary as we rolled along. Quietly into my ear as I talked, the official identified each building we passed, each group of applauding citizens, each forest of decorations. But I was aware that he did not speak when we were passing the biggest Union Jack of all, flying above a large wooden house which although undistinguished was evidently important. In front of the place, a group of women stood cheering immoderately. I nudged my helper and made an inquiring gesture towards the place. He seemed reluctant to answer, but whispered:

'Don't mention for BBC. That house is – er, well, it is a resort of pleasure. But, you see, all the ladies are most loyal.'

If memory serves, it was later in that tour that the Duke of Edinburgh, for once in his life, was taken aback and momentarily at a loss for words. We were on a Caribbean island and it was a routine scene: the Queen and her husband were standing side by side under the blazing sun in a viceregal garden and a large number of local worthies were coming forward one by one to be presented and to have their hands shaken. All the presentees were proud to have this moment of glory: the bows were low, the curtseys deep. None so deep as that of an ample lady who performed in front of Her Majesty an obeisance so low that at the end of it she collapsed with a plonk, her large print behind resting on the ground. Assisted to her feet, she took a pace to her left, to be presented now to the Duke. She was feeling embarrassed, as well she might be; and His Royal Highness, at pains to resore her composure, put out his hand, smiled in a most kindly way, and warmly spoke the customary 'How d'you do?' At which, the lady, still somewhat flustered, tossed her head and replied: 'I am married!' – and flounced off the stage.

Prince Philip's jaw dropped, but no riposte came. It was the only time I have seen that very articulate man bereft of speech.

We were on a long passage through the West Indies then. It was a tour full of delights, especially the exciting music. The sound of a full Trinidad carnival – even without the rainbow sight of it – has to be heard to be believed; the calypso kings, with names such as Mighty Sparrow, King Cobra and Lord Kitchener, are a race apart; and the Caribbean steel bands, the good ones, are makers of rare concert sounds. Before I went to the islands I thought that a steel band was just a primitive deafening noise that went on interminably during nightlong 'jump ups'. How was I to know, until I watched them being made and tuned and until I recorded their playing 'on site', that sawn-off oil drums in the hands of music-loving West Indians can become pure orchestral instruments of enchanting tone? I put on to my recording tapes some steel band selections which I found at the time, and still find, magnificently moving. I had expected the swelling volume, but not the delicacy. I didn't imagine that the Hallelujah Chorus could be rendered in such a hauntingly beautiful manner as it was by those unlettered island boys sitting on the ground and hitting tin tubs.

I could never, on the other hand, bring myself to enjoy the music of the East. And never disliked it more than when I struggled with it in India. On one visit to the subcontinent I was in Delhi and had a good story to send to London. But when I arrived at All India Radio to put over my dispatch I found the studio which I had booked was packed to the walls with musicians sitting on the floor and twanging mightily. It took so long to get them sorted out and to find another studio for me that when I called Broadcasting House nobody in London was listening: they had become tired of waiting and cancelled the Delhi circuit for the day. Music never had fewer charms!

In Ahmedabad, India's textile city, I rushed into the local studios with an urgent eye-witness story of riots. This time London, via Poona, was eagerly waiting, but the transmission was ruined by a band of flute players enthusiastically rehearsing in the corridor just outside my far-from-soundproof studio door, and I had to stop my talk and go out and attempt to beg a little hush. The mad Englishman's protests were met only with smiles and renewed playing, however. They kept pausing briefly, but evidently only to gather strength, for each time I began to repeat my dispatch the cacophony burst forth again after a few sentences. In the end, only a threat and a bribe brought my needed five minutes of peace.

Next it was Pakistan; and that country produced episodes which would have made the Marx Brothers jealous. I started my 'Hello London!' from a studio in Karachi one day and was well into my news report – 'live' into a programme, as it happened – when suddenly the studio door was flung open admitting a strong draught and a wizened man in a little cap and a long coat. He entered backwards addressing a crowd of babbling people who came surging in after him as he cried: 'This, friends, is what we call a talks studio.' Listeners in Britain must have heard him quite clearly. He was conducting visitors on a tour of the building – and no one had switched on the red 'In Use' warning-light outside my studio. Still holding my script with one hand and waving angrily at the man to go away, I continued with my talk as best I could. It seemed to take a long time for the chap to realize his error, and even when he did, the idea that I might be speaking 'live' to an important audience did not seem to have occurred to him. For before he led his flock out he came giggling across to my table and said – to the microphone as well as to me – 'Oh dear me, let me be excused. Forgive this foolish person.'

In London they were rocking with laughter. Such a nice change, they said. My Karachi spot had brightened their day. But not mine.

I ought not, I suppose, to have been surprised at what happened later in Rawalpindi, again at a radio station. I was in the middle of my broadcast there – in a very un-studiolike room with a fireplace and easy chairs – when an aged bearer tottered happily in and proceeded to poke the fire with a prodigious banging and clattering. The niceties of broadcasting seemed to be lost on him, and although he apologized he looked surprised to be shoved out of the room. Perhaps it was to make amends that, before I had finished my piece, he came shambling in again, bowing and smiling into his beard, and this time banging a tray of tea on the table beside the microphone, very noisily too. His manner suggested a view that, whatever nonsense the lunatic at the microphone was up to, he would be better for a dish of char.

It was when I went south to Ceylon, the Sri Lanka of today, that I was put into the most unlikely 'studio'. They provided me with a microphone in the heart of the Temple of the Tooth in Kandy, the old hill city which was the last capital of the Sinhalese kings. This is the temple in which is enshrined the dental relic which, they say, is a tooth of the holy Buddha himself. To my astonishment, when I arrived at the temple one sweltering evening some local radio engineers were running lines far inside the building. They assured me that a microphone for my use was already within. The reason for this special treatment – as so often – was not any personal charm or commanding presence of mine: it was that some of the importance of the people whose doings I was reporting had rubbed off on to me. I was travelling through Ceylon with the entourage of the Queen and Prince Philip, and they were coming to see this famous and venerated temple. So there I was, with a circuit to London arranged thanks to Radio Ceylon, half an hour before the official arrival. Not only that: the chief priest invited me to come into the inner shrine and watch, and describe, the uncovering of the sacred relic. Few people have ever seen the tooth. And no wonder. It is normally kept encased within fantastic cocoons of priceless gems.

The unveiling was a solemn, prescribed ceremony. Having removed my shoes, I was led from the thickly carpeted court of the temple through doors inlaid with ivory and silver and up a twisting flight of stairs to the Chamber of the Tooth, a round and elaborately bedizened room. Into this holy of holies there entered in silent procession a body of Buddhist monks, shaven headed and wearing long saffron robes, one of whom slowly unlocked the gate of an iron-barred cage which stood floodlit in the centre of the chamber. His companions removed the bars, and a series of glass panels, to disclose a tall casket, higher than a man, shaped like a bell and hung about with scores of gold chains. But there was not only one casket. Pairs of priests set to work, in a reverent manner with many pauses and bows but also with what seemed to be a well rehearsed drill, and lifted off casing after casing.

All this, astonished and not well versed in what was happening, I tried to describe into the microphone which had been politely handed to me when first I entered the chamber. The proceedings were like an Arabian Nights dream. Each casket lifted off by the priests disclosed a slightly smaller one – and each made of gold and silver studded with gems – until at last, after a ceremony which had lasted half an hour, a small and exquisitely fashioned ornament was revealed. This I saw to be a golden stand in yet another glass case; and in it, held up by a gold ring on the stem of a lotus flower also made of gold, was – The Tooth.

It was thick and a full three inches long. Not human.

However, that object is what the Queen came and saw and duly marvelled at. The whole business was very strange, the temple scene both mystic and modern, for the Queen and Prince Philip seemed quite incongruous figures in the centre of the ancient ritual, she in Hartnell gown and tiara and he in white tie and tails. Buddhism too had been on ceremonial parade and, if we did not that night achieve Nirvana, we at any rate saw things which seemed out of this world.

For the temple call was immediately followed by another unusual experience in which bygone pageantry returned briefly to the old city. This was a *Raja Perahera*, a great festival procession staged for the Queen and her husband who sat watching it all from a special perch beside a main street in the centre of Kandy, a newly built pavilion near the palace of the old kings. They saw The Tooth borne in procession. First of all there came, slowly and ponderously through roadways thronged on either side by thousands of people roaring applause, the elephants – hundreds of them – elephants filling the street as far as you could see; elephants of every size from nervous babies to giant creatures with tusks encased in gold; elephants fantastically caparisoned and hung with tinkling bells; elephants with flowers painted on their vast rumps; elephants carrying their own illuminations, blazing electric bulbs which outlined heads, trunks, flapping ears and the howdahs in which sat, richly costumed, the high personages of Kandy; elephants driven by mahouts astride the animals' necks and carrying decorated shields and tall fans. Next came Kandyan chiefs walking along the road in groups, every man in golden slippers, stately and splendid in cloth of gold and bearing jewelled swords and daggers. On the fingers of their hands, which they waved above their heads to acknowledge the greeting of the crowds, were bundles of the heaviest rings I have ever seen.

The *Perahera* went on for two hours. The weather was still terribly hot even when midnight came, and, to add to the sweat from my forehead, my eyes began to stream in irritation at the thick clouds of smoke which presently enveloped the procession and all the watchers. The smoke was from a hundred marching men carrying flaming torches; and they in turn were followed by scores of capering figures who cracked long whips with tremendous noise as they went along, and by dancers leaping up and down to show off their jingling silver ornaments and grotesque headdresses. The ear-splitting sound of it all matched the exotic sight. Films and photographs could not adequately compass it; certainly my commentary couldn't, though I tried.

After the exhaustions of the tour through Ceylon, I hoped that the broadcast I had to do on the travellers' departure from Ceylon would be comparatively easy. But not a bit of it. The departure was from Colombo in the S S *Gothic*, temporarily the royal yacht, in which I was accompanying the party as commentator. As the ship sailed, commentaries were made from the shore and from me on the *Gothic*'s poop; and all went merrily. Then when the yacht had cleared the breakwater and was heading out into the Indian Ocean, my job was to go below and, on a cue given by broadcasters still describing events on the quayside, speak the next part of the programme to the listening world from Her Majesty's own stateroom. The Queen had chosen to broadcast her farewell to Ceylon from her departing ship at sea – on her twenty-eighth birthday – and I had to introduce the royal speech.

So the scene was the spacious day-cabin of the Sovereign, with one of our BBC microphones set up on the Queen's desk and in front of it the Queen herself, script at the ready, sitting cool and relaxed in a simple summer frock. As the time drew near when we might expect our signal to start, I stood at another microphone in a corner of the saloon and waited, headphones on, listening to the shore for the cue-over to the *Gothic*. But, alas, it never came. There was a click in my earpieces, and then silence: we had lost the link. Nothing my engineering colleague on board could do was effective in restoring communication from shore to ship: *we* could broadcast, but could not *receive* a sound. I did not know what to do. Were they still broadcasting from the quay or had they, already given the cue to me? If I waited, I might be launching the Queen's voice into the world's ether only after a period of dreadful silence during which listeners would have switched off; but if I started now, 'blind', it might mean that she would be talking over somebody else still speaking from the shore.

As I waited in my corner, perspiring with nervousness and dilemma, Her Majesty looked across with eyebrows raised inquiringly, wondering what was happening and when we were going to begin. Prince Philip put his head round the door and said: 'What's happened to the wireless?' I made a helpless gesture, took hold of the microphone, and plunged into my announcement, signalled the Queen to start, and sank down in a chair to listen to a quite unruffled speech. I made a closing announcement (I was told my face was still a picture of agony), and rushed off to conduct an inquest with Radio Ceylon over the ordinary ship's wireless. Colombo were suspiciously vague in their answers, then admitted that somebody at the radio must have mistakenly pulled out a plug and silenced the shore broadcast. But it turned out that I had made a lucky guess with the timing: the broadcast from the royal stateroom had gone out loud and clear and at the right moment.

That was the only time the Queen's cabin was my studio, though I had to make a number of broadcasts from the ship during the six-month trip I had in the *Gothic* when the Queen went round the world in the vessel soon after her Coronation. The funniest commentary I made, though, was never broadcast publicly at all. I made it on to discs during the 'crossing the line' frolics on board, which were led by Prince Philip, in dirty shorts and a butcher's apron, playing the part of the Barber and indulging a talent for horseplay as he tipped the initiates at King Neptune's court into our little well-deck swimming pool. He saw to it that everybody who had not crossed the equator before received a ducking: ladies in waiting, equerries, footmen and Privy Purse typists were treated with impartial gusto. The Queen, with her small ciné-camera, filmed the best episodes of the performance. I recorded a description – and the screams and shouts. Next day there was repeat laughter when my commentary was played over the ship's loudspeaker system. It was a somewhat rough-hewn description. I had made it while standing precariously near the edge of the pool, and every other sentence seemed to be punctuated by my involuntary exclamations of 'Whoops!'

I made a less happy recording during that voyage, in mid-Pacific, standing on deck and holding my microphone aloft in order to get on disc the sound of *Gothic*'s siren. The BBC wanted the noise to include in a Christmas Day round-the-world programme. I had obtained royal permission for the ship's hooter to be sounded – it was a very loud and startling noise indeed – in all sorts of combinations of long and short blasts, simply for my benefit; and a warning memorandum had been sent round to everybody on board so that none would be taken by surprise by the hooter giving danger signals.

But the notice from the Queen that some unusual sounds would be heard at eleven o'clock on that particular morning had not apparently reached the Queen's husband. For when the siren began its deep reverberating blasts that made the whole ship shudder, a secretary came tearing down to me crying: 'For God's sake, what's happening? Stop the noise; tell the captain. Prince Philip is dictating letters and can't hear himself speak.' At the same moment two strange figures appeared on deck: two maids attached to the royal household could be seen running towards one of the ship's lifeboat stations, each lady clutching a bundle of clothing and wearing a life-vest. They too had not received the warning about the siren, and had interpreted the hooting as a signal of emergency and were prepared to abandon ship.

I was not popular then on board the *Gothic*. But Prince Philip allowed me three minutes' play with the noises. And the Queen laughed.

I imagine that the funniest sight I ever presented was when I was playing Broadcaster Afloat aboard a very different craft: a war canoe. It was in Nigeria and I was crouching, with a portable recorder in my lap, at the sharp end of a huge canoe which was in a flotilla of overloaded tubs parading in front of royalty on the muddy waters of the Bonny at Port Harcourt, in the region of deltas and mangrove swamps which are part of the Rivers Province. Behind me, all in our one frail craft, were forty armed paddlers, four drummers, a naked figure manning an old Portuguese cannon, and on a platform two chiefs carrying flags, one man dressed in a funeral top hat and the other wearing a Victorian fire helmet. The voyagers in our canoe and others of the amazing fleet paddled up and down chanting and yelling and discharging hundreds of old rifles in a non-stop *feu de joie*. It was a remarkable sight. Best of all, for certain of the spectators on the river banks, was the spectacle of me, an incongruous figure in sweat-stained bush shirt among all the undressed warriors, trying to talk and keep my balance in the din and the dithering of my rocking vessel. A great shout of laughter went up when we had a collision and I was shot off my perch and fell into the river, still talking. The recording machine suffered far more than I did.

Of course there were plenty of dull moments on these tours, but it is always the bright lights one remembers. And there were plenty of those too – enough for me always to be eager for the next journey. Indeed, sitting in studios in London and reporting from a cosy and well equipped Broad-casting House felt a little 'stale, flat and unprofitable' between whiles. When the next assignment beckoned, I was ready, though well aware that some of its talking-places would be less comfortable.

I once made the driver's box high up on a crane my 'studio'. That was in Liberia, the black 'Little America' on the steamy west coast of Africa, a Negro dollar-republic founded as a home for freed slaves under the patronage of the United States. Liberia, however, has long ago become rich, indepen-dent and possessed of a consciously 'civilized' capital city; and it was a modern-looking scene that I looked down on from my eagle's-nest in Monrovia that morning. I was doing a commentary on the arrival of the Queen's ship – it was the *Britannia* now – in Monrovia's spacious man-made harbour.

The entry of the yacht did not quite go according to sched-ule. The *Britannia* was being escorted by the yacht of another Head of State, the Queen's host, the ebullient William Shadrach Tubman, who had already been President of Liberia for seven-teen years, an African extrovert and father-figure, shrewd but outgoing, and very much the ruler of the country. Tubman (who died in 1971) was then a lively and endearing character, a speech-making, hymn-singing autocrat, proud to be a des-cendant of American slaves, inordinately fond of dressing in formal black jacket, striped trousers, white spats, plus ebony cane and Havana cigar. It would have been strange if such a man *didn't* have a presidential yacht; strange if he hadn't gone out to meet the Queen in it. Of course he did.

On this particular morning the British yacht came in first and was lying in the centre of the haven – fortunately still on the alert and under power – when the Tubman vessel came tearing in. Evidently actuated by the President's mettlesome spirit, it entered harbour like a speedboat, steering an erratic course and making straight for the *Britannia*. But the royal ship was not rammed: it took evasive action.

This was a diverting spectacle from the top of my crane. But I have no doubt the manoeuvre was a shade too unorthodox for Flag Officer Royal Yachts.

At length Mr Tubman came ashore and waited on the waterside for his guests to land from the royal barge. Looking down on the Liberian reception line-up, I felt hotter than ever. The weather was ninety in the shade and sultry, but Mr Tubman and his Cabinet were standing out there in the full blast of the sun, each man clad in a thick dark tailcoat of European winter weight and heavily hatted and gloved. Full dress was the order of the day – and no concessions to the climate. Yet the President was the picture of ease and energy. He walked up and down waving his arms about and patting people on the back; his shining black face was one huge beam. When the Queen did arrive – in a thin summer dress, and Philip in tropical white – the man was wellnigh airborne with joy and only just stopped himself from kissing his visitors.

There followed a procession through the lively streets of Monrovia, streets lined by stars-and-stripes flags, soldiers looking like dark GIs, and gum-chewing, whistle-blowing cops who might have come straight out of New York. True to the American style of Monrovia, the drive ended, not at a town hall but in front of the 'Executive Mansion', the vast new official residence of Mr T. While the visitors were inside there, being offered highballs, old-fashioneds and scotch-on-the-rocks, it was almost a relief to those of us remaining outside to be reminded that we were still in Africa by a flock of devil-dancers clothed in leopard skins who came capering and drum walloping in front of the building. I was told they were primitives who had trekked in from the hinterland to see the White Queen – though I would not have been surprised if they'd turned out to be a cabaret troupe which government hospitality had organized for the occasion from some Liberian Las Vegas up the road.

But that night, when I had to take some BBC tapes and film to be shipped from the airport, I knew without doubt that we were in a strange wild land. The airport of Monrovia, Roberts Field, is fifty miles from the city, fifty miles of black, pot-holed tarmac highway streaking through the thick trees of endless rubber plantations, the forests of Firestone. I was driven at breakneck speed by a chuckling African in a powerful open car, a Detroit monster, once beautiful but now battered and rattling. My chauffeur never swerved when we met oncoming vehicles – they just had to take to the forest verges – and after a while I shut my eyes and prayed. It was not surprising that the roadsides were littered by hundreds of smashed Pontiacs and Chevrolets which, having crashed, were simply left to rust and rot. In Liberia as well as America, cars are expendables.

The radio station I used was up a turning halfway along that road: Station ELWA. I was told that only from this station had I any hope of getting through to London, for it had a powerful transmitter. The station proved to be a collection of huts in a clearing. Called the Radio Village, it was a missionary station, a remote mouthpiece of the Sudan Interior Mission. I was warmly greeted by a rumpled man in an old khaki vest and frayed shorts, who sat me down on a verandah under a large fan, placed an iced lime juice at my elbow and asked me to wait a few minutes until he had switched on the transmitter and opened their own broadcast programme (which meant that he read a news bulletin and a passage from the Bible and then put on a long-playing disc of hymns). 'Call me Al,' he said. 'I do most things round here.' He was in fact a Lutheran pastor, who ran a medical centre as well as the radio.

At length I took my place at his microphone and began calling England: 'Hello London. This is Eee Ell Doubleyou Aye, Liberia!' Al interrupted me and suggested that it might be easier for anyone to pick us up and identify where we were calling from if I spoke, in full, the name which the call-sign letters ELWA had come to stand for. 'We ran a competition,' he said, 'and listeners were invited to make a name out of our code letters. The best entry was "Eternal Love Winning Africa" and it's always what the station is called now.'

And that is how I came to astonish a listening BBC by starting my Liberian dispatches with: 'This is Godfrey Talbot in eternal love winning Africa.'

They gave me one of their fat hymnbooks and a tape of ELWA prayers as mementoes when I left that hospitable outpost of evangelism. On getting back into Monrovia I discovered that the Queen too had been given unusual presents just before she sailed away. Her gifts, like mine, were to be shipped to London later. Which was a good thing, because one of the presents Mr Tubman gave her was a baby hippopotamus.

A week later, on leaving Bathurst after a call on The Gambia, Her Majesty received another wildlife gift; but this one did *not* travel separately when she sailed. It was a crocodile, passed on board at the last minute in a metal box full of ventilation holes. Nobody knew what it was until the yacht was out at sea. The royal household had not had quite this sort of reptile problem before; but the Queen has a devoted staff: the crocodile made the passage to the next port, Dakar, in her private secretary's bath.

Speaking of baths, I once made a studio out of my bathroom. It was in Edinburgh during a royal visit there. I was staying in the North British Hotel and as my bedroom, which had a small balcony and a small bathroom, overlooked Princes Street and the route of processions I had to describe, I had the microphone placed on the balcony and looked forward to a comfortable and convenient vantage point. But my balcony was too insecure as an OB point, so I retreated to the bathroom next door and broadcast whilst standing in the tub and looking through the open window. My voice echoed a bit, but the balance of sound from the streets was just right.

In Edinburgh I once made a terrible mistake – not on the air, but it was embarrassing all the same. Back in 1953, I was covering the Coronation state visit to the Scottish capital and, after attending the great service of celebration in St Giles' Cathedral, I rushed round to the Signet Library at the back of the church to find a telephone and get through to London with a report for the One o'Clock News. I had to fight my way through clutters of Scottish peers in full flowing regalia who were using the library to disrobe in. I reached the Signet office in a testy state, and was even more annoyed to find the room locked up for the day and its telephones unattainable.

I rounded on a mild-looking man in a sober suit who was standing watching the scenery from a doorway – an office worker, I guessed – and snapped at him: 'Can you get me one of your phones, quick, please. I shall miss the BBC bulletin at this rate. There are three phones across the way, but these wretched dressed-up peers are hogging the lines. Can you not do something?'

With an air of self-reproach, the man answered: 'Sorry, I can't do anything. Not here. If I were at home, I'd like fine for you to have the line.'

Well, he still might help, I thought. Perhaps he lived only just up the street. So I said: 'Where's your home?'

'Glamis . . . My name's Strathmore.'

Collapse of BBC correspondent. For I was addressing the sixteenth Earl of Strathmore and Kinghorne, master of Glamis Castle, cousin of the Queen. He had changed out of *his* peer's robes early. A kind man. Far from being offended at me, he led me to a vacant phone-box in the High Street.

The encounter was useful in the fullness of time, for one day, forgiven and welcomed, I took a news film crew to Glamis – and had free use of a baronial telephone. . . .

Looking through piles of notebooks and diaries I have kept over the years, undeniably a great deal of my professional life has been spent in calling 'Hello London!' from great houses and palaces which are the 'tied cottages' of royalty, and in broadcasting from dignified and predictable state corroborees. I was sometimes in danger of being type-cast as a courtier – the diaries bear that out. But there was always general reporting too: political stories, interviews, air disasters, international conferences, strikes, murders and sudden death. Nor were the assignments always serious ones. In the middle of reporting some horseback Olympic Games in Sweden I was required to act as dance-band compère at a ball which was being broadcast from a Stockholm palace and which provided a hilarious evening. I have nothing but the most affectionate memories of standing on a piano and sharing the announcing with the Latin American maestro, Edmundo Ros (who could teach anybody how to keep going a flow of words as well as a flow of music).

There is also a memory of Beirut in happier days, when I made some recordings very different from my familiar line. My real mission in the Lebanon had been concerned with the antiquities of Tyre and Sidon, Baalbek and the Cedars, but a BBC 'Holiday Hour' programme asked for a 'sound picture' of lighter Lebanese attractions, the music and the night clubs for instance. Could I do something of the sort? Certainly, said an eager Tourist Department, to which I had to turn; and I was whisked to a kind of Sunset Strip beside the Mediterranean. So I spent one eventful night communicating from a cabaret in a large casino north of the capital. My colleague and I were planted at a table at the very edge of a vast stage which, when the entertainment came, was shaken by the concerted leaps and crashes of a juicy Moulin Rouge chorus doing the splits at high speed. We were almost personally involved, recording apparatus and cameras almost too close, for the involuntary grunts of the acrobatic ladies were audible on our magnetic tape, the darns in their tights plain on our film. Whilst the act was on, we felt as though we were under a sort of artillery barrage of showgirls. But we soldiered on, fortified by the proprietor's champagne and stimulated by the breezes set up by the lifting of can-can skirts and the close flapping of two-inch eyelashes as the beautiful Ginette and Monique and the rest squealed down the very throat of the microphone.

That evening – in the days when Beirut was not war-torn, but was the Paris of the Middle East – came vividly back recently when I found in an old Beirut notebook a name written in lipstick and three wisps of a feather boa pressed between the pages.

I should have liked somehow to get an echo of that cabaret sound into the programme which Roy Plomley made when I was dignified by being the castaway in 'Desert Island Discs', for your business in such a programme is to look back on your work in music and words. But, inevitably, they wanted me to take the lid off royal occasions, not knockabout nights on the coast of Phoenicia.

'Desert Island Discs' is hardly ever broadcast 'live'. But my edition was – from a studio like a goldfish bowl too: the programme went out direct and unrehearsed from a glass-walled room at the Radio and Television Show at the Earls Court exhibition centre in London. Plomley gracefully said he wouldn't have done it 'live' if he hadn't had a 'pro' as victim. He had, in me, an old hand at the Hello Business.

Alamein in England

Being a veteran is valuable.

One of the pleasures of my trade of licensed witness is that your memory, your personal nostalgia, becomes increasingly useful professionally as the years go by. As long as you like broadcasting, experience of men and affairs is a bonus and a practical asset when the anniversaries come, when peaks from the century's history are affectionately celebrated, and when great men pass away. At such moments my telephone at home rings and the voice of a news editor says: 'You knew So-and-So in his prime, didn't you?' or 'I believe you were present when the actual event took place, so can you come in and do us a four-minute piece for "The World at One"?' Or it may be: 'We'd like to interview you in tonight's "Nationwide".'

I have no illusions on these occasions that the callers are flattering me. No, programme producers are dispassionate beavers, not philanthropists. I know some of these hawks who would drag their ancient grandmothers out of sickbeds at midnight if they thought there was a broadcastable story in them. What a news programme wants when a story breaks is an immediate interview with a reasonably articulate authority, an eye-witness, someone with first-hand acquaintance or special memory of the happening or person suddenly become a head-line (not, that is, a chap who would have to look up newspaper clippings and write a script before facing microphone and camera). That is why (and there is an instance at the end of Chapter 13) an urgent ring sometimes summons me.

But old associations have brought me predictable as well as unexpected broadcasts. Often I have covered the annual

Alamein Reunion, which assiduously cherishes echoes of war and wartime comradeship. They still go on, these Desert Rats' get-togethers, each October on the anniversary of the battle. The great night at the Royal Festival Hall beside the Thames is always a complete 'sell out' and three thousand people fill the place. Old Eighth Army men apply for tickets early, proudly giving their army numbers and the names of the formations they were in at the time of the offensive. The soldiers of a quarter of a century ago are now middle-aged and more, men with too little hair and too much tummy: but you can see them pushing their chests out and squaring their shoulders as they come smiling into the hall to meet their old pals and have a few beers with them. Thirty thousand bottles of ale are dispatched at each gathering.

But it is not a raucus sentimental binge. Wives and sons and sons' girl friends are present too, and there is dancing at the end of the evening. There is ritual, rousing military band music, community singing, a music hall act or two, a general's speech, a message from the Queen, and 'Land of Hope and Glory'. It is like a Festival of Remembrance, an Aldershot Tattoo and a Last Night of the Proms rolled into one. A resolute seriousness and a sense of united-purpose comes over the company when the drums roll, the spotlight shines on the huge Union Jack and Eighth Army star and shield, and the divisional standards are marched on to the stage to roars of applause. This is always a special moment for the old sweats of the Desert Army: Alamein was their Agincourt, and this the St Crispin's Day on which they are again a band of brothers.

For twenty years after the war it was, naturally, Field Marshal Montgomery, their old commander, who made the speech; then, as Monty became very old and infirm (he died in 1976 at 88), it was his successor Sir Oliver Leese, and others, who came on stage and spoke the applauded tribute to the Alamein spirit. But it is the appearance of Vera Lynn – 'Sweetheart of the Forces', now Dame Vera – which brings the house down. Year after year she comes and sings the old songs: 'We'll Meet Again' and 'White Cliffs of Dover'.

One year there was an additional songstress: Marlene Dietrich, with whom the Eighth Army's 'Lilli Marlene' is now associated (though, as a matter of history, it was not she but an actress on the Nazi radio who sang the song in 1942). Miss Dietrich was the special attraction of the Reunion of 1963, the twenty-first anniversary of the battle, staged on that occasion in the Albert Hall. I had to do a commentary from the evening's entertainment and, to get the feel of the show, attended the afternoon rehearsal. This was distinguished by the behaviour of Miss Dietrich, a very professional person in a sort of Dior boiler-suit, who marched up and down the stage issuing her requirements to producer, musical director, limelight men and all and sundry.

In the middle of the rehearsal Lord Montgomery walked in to see how things were going. I wanted to interview both the soldier and the star, so after the lady had gone through the drill for her act I introduced her to Monty and popped them both into the box which the BBC has at the Albert Hall, permanently wired and equipped. I put the microphone in front of them, set a recording machine going, and got them to interview each other. The result was diverting. Marlene had never met anyone like Monty before, and Monty had not met many actresses, certainly nobody like this one. Marlene put out a finger and prodded the Field Marshal in the chest in the middle of the dazzling square of medal ribbons on his battle-dress coat, and asked him about the decorations. He replied at some length and, slightly nervously regarding the curves which were the decorations of *her* battledress, inquired about her German origin, asking why she had become an American. She looked at him with gentle pity, patted his knee, and answered: 'Money, dahling, money.'

Monty, I remember, was a little taken aback by this familiarity, but soon recovered his perkiness and began telling La Dietrich about his victories and his beliefs – and even his views on the theatre. He always had a penchant for telling others how to do their business, as I had rediscovered when, a short time before that anniversary I went down to his home, near Alton in Hampshire, to talk to him in a special interview he had agreed to give for radio and television. He was then a mere seventy-five years old and very spry, long accustomed to being the most famous, perhaps the most notorious, certainly the most publicized, British soldier since the Duke of Wellington.

The Field Marshal's home was a converted mill-house, very pleasant and in most agreeable country; and we were doing the interview in the orchard of his garden, where all the young trees stood to attention in immaculate lines and every bit of grass was almost indecently tidy – he used to issue orders that there should be no weeds seen in either the garden or the mill stream.

At the interview I had to restrain him from telling the cameraman where to stand and me how to hold the microphone. He was impatient to start, and when I said we wanted the interview to be no longer than seven minutes he retorted: 'That's all right. Leave it to me. I'm experienced in this broadcast-timing business. Let's get on with it.'

He was very good, and talked in his most confident and controversial manner in answer to my questions, telling the world and its political leaders how they should behave and giving caustic comments on modern youth and pert young military historians. When at length he stopped and we switched off the camera and recording tapes he said: 'That will do nicely, I think, Talbot. Very good, wasn't I?' I agreed that he was, but had to add that, in spite of his promise to keep an eye on his watch, he had gone on far too long, twelve minutes, and the film and recording would have to be cut. Monty was in no way disconcerted at this, and as usual had a simple solution:

'That's an easy problem, my boy. It's me they want to hear, not you. Cut out your questions, leave in my answers, and we'll be home and dry.'

I have had to interview many other egotists; and they always produced problems. Another once very self-confident figure – who has now passed from the front pages and from life itself – was the Emperor Haile Selassie of Ethiopia, who ruled in Addis Ababa with the absolute power of an autocrat for half a century before he was savagely removed. I had met him during his wartime exile in Britain and marvelled at his fierce-eyed dignity – he certainly behaved like 'the Elect of God'. I talked to him again, in the post-war years and well before his brutal deposition and death, at his palace in Addis. I had worked hard to secure an audience and was told it was a rare privilege to see him, for His Imperial Majesty was almost a god: I often saw people in the streets lying down and rubbing their foreheads in the dust when his car passed.

On the day of the interview I got a shock. Having passed the soldiers of the Imperial Guard at the gates and gained the pillared portico of the palace, a small, black-bearded, bemedalled figure in uniform advanced towards me – and at his side, also making for me, was a lion, a very growlingly real full-grown one. The Emperor was holding the beast loosely on what seemed to me an all-too-slender chain. 'This,' he said, 'is Tojo, my favourite. You may see more lions in cages in the compound. I am a keeper of lions.' I knew that one of His Majesty's many titles was 'Lion of Judah', but I thought that to walk about with jungle cats was carrying things to far, and I was to terrified to unfurl the microphone. Fortunately, the Emperor, having displayed his pet, allowed a bodyguard to lead Tojo away, and we then got on with the interview. He talked well, frequently breaking into French, and dilated on many topics, including his hopes of African unity. In the end we ran out of tape and it was clear that the interview would have to be edited down to a suitable length, for he had rambled on and on almost without pause. I didn't dare tell him this – though *he* couldn't have said 'Cut out the interviewer's voice': the interviewer had hardly got a word in.

I have often been in the same situation when interviewing personalities of the stage and screen. Reticence, of course, is not their business and, being 'full of themselves', the sight of microphone and camera frequently triggers a flow of non-stop talk veering far off the subject in hand. Quickness and firmness is needed to get them back on the rails. It is both fascinating and challenging to try to contain, within the few minutes allowed for the usual interview, the surging fluency of certain politicians. Lord George-Brown has for long been an example of the public figure who is never at a loss for words and who, given a spot in a 'chat show', shows every sign of filling the entire programme with his views.

Harold Macmillan is easy with words, but in a different class, urbanity itself. To interview him is sheer pleasure; and the temptation is to sit back and listen for ever to the suavity and elegant wit of the veteran statesman, to the rich reminiscences, the acute and uniquely entertaining observations he makes on the famous people and famous episodes of his long and distinguished life. In old age and retirement from the political fight he has become a more brilliant talker than ever. Somehow, we never realized what a television star was to develop long after his years of ministerial office – though I must say I always found him relaxed and unflappable at the microphone. I cherish the memory of him at London Airport one day beginning a 'live' statement, and an important one, with the words: 'Goodness, what a lot of cameras! Shall I start now?'

On quite another tack, I have never laughed so much in an interview as I did when confronting Mae West, an overwhelming 'Diamond Lil' ogling me out of a nest of white furs and making outrageous gestures with the microphone which she had taken from my hand. She dismissed from the room her three attendant gag-writers with a drawled 'Get lost, boys', and proceeded to be very funny indeed without being told what to say. I was surprised to find her knowledgeable about politics and books and music; but she was at her typical best, of course, when she was rattling away about the theatre and the parts she had played – and hadn't played: 'Always wanted to be Delilah,' she purred. 'The only woman barber who made good.'

To interview Noël Coward – if you could, and once I did – was to have the rapier wit confirmed, and devastating cracks aimed at the interviewer so wickedly that every question you put was made to sound banal. Coward was the sharpest talker I ever heard (Sir Cecil Beaton now runs him close): he did not need pen and paper and meditation to be funny. Instant sallies bubbled from his conversation.

There was an example of this on the day of the Queen's Coronation in 1953 when, with a number of fellow spirits, he was on a club balcony watching the procession of open carriages driving from Westminster Abbey to Buckingham Palace. One of the great sights of that rain-soaked cavalcade was the eighteen-stone Queen Salote of Tonga, a magnificent Polynesian lady six feet four inches in height, smiling fit to burst, sitting bolt upright in a landau whose only other occupant was a tiny Sultan from the Malay Straits, a human being a quarter of her size. As the carriage rolled by beneath the club window, a voice from the spectators up there, powered by champagne, fluted: 'Who on earth is that woman?' When one of the inquirer's companions told him it was the Sovereign of Tonga and he replied, 'Who's that riding with her?' Noël Coward chirped out with: 'Dear boy, it's her lunch of course.'

That South Pacific queen was, as well he knew, a cultured and highly Western-civilized lady, the antithesis of a cannibal. But he couldn't resist the crack.

Salote died in 1965, and has been succeeded by another remarkable personality, her eldest son who is now His Majesty King Taufa Ahau Tupou the Fourth and rules as an independent sovereign over those tropical Tongan islands. I first met him at his palace home in Nukualofa when his mother was reigning and he was Crown Prince Tungi. Not long ago, when he was visiting London as a king, but privately, I met him again and this time had a congenial interview with him. He invited me to bring the microphone along.

It was very clear that this son was mightier than his famous mother in one respect: he was five stones heavier – at twenty-three stones certainly the greatest king on earth. In Tonga it is regarded as desirable to be of large proportions, and I am sure that the size of the King commands great respect. He told me, without embarrassment, that his vital statistics were 54–52–59, and his collar size 23 inches.

The King's mind, I found, possessed an agility his body could not have. It was a master of languages, the law, mathematics, teacher training and international diplomacy. He was something of a musician too. At least he had an infectious fondness for simple melodies, for the folk tunes of his native islands, and for old Wesleyan hymns. He was as good a hymn singer as his late mother, whom I had seen heading a thunderous congregation inside the big white Methodist church in Tongatapu less than a year after she had paid her well-remembered vist to London in 1953.

That queen's son not only talked and sang for me but played as well. A small electric organ had been installed for him in the house in Belgravia where he was staying, for playing the organ is one of his recreations. He thumped away with unaffected ardour, a book of Moody and Sankey gospel numbers propped up in front of him, and encouraged me to record the sound. This I did, regretting that I could not take a photograph also. The sight of the monarch seated upon a wide organ bench was remarkable: the bench was wholly obliterated by his ample posterior, and in fact there was a bit of king beyond either end.

He talked, during the recorded interview, about his own generous physical proportions; and, incidentally, I helped him with one of his weight problems, in an unexpected way. He mentioned a few of the things he was doing in London, and added that there were a couple of films in the West End in which he was interested but which, in his words, 'I am sure I cannot see.'

'Why not, Your Majesty?' I asked, quite innocently, but thinking that perhaps the pictures in question were too raw for Methodist eyes.

The King looked at me as one does an obtuse child, and answered slowly and deliberately: 'I cannot fit into the cinema seats.'

I ought to have known. I was impressed enough with the size of him. Anyhow, we went on to talk of many other things; and when the evening ended I drove to the BBC with my tapes. They were patiently listened to by producers and editors of the 'Today' programme, and at breakfast time next morning extracts from the conversation were broadcast, including the bit about no film-going.

As a result, the telephones in my office in Broadcasting House began buzzing with calls from cinema managers who had heard the remark and were anxious to have Salote's son in their theatres whatever his shape. Because of their offers and suggestions, the King did manage to see both the films of his desire. At one cinema they put a special chair out for him; at another, there were still a few of those double seats which used to be so popular with courting couples some two decades ago, and one such seat accommodated Tonga's king – just.

His Majesty was in true tradition. Watching films has long

been a royal habit. The British Royal Family's interest in the cinema is not confined to attendances at gala premières for charity. Private viewings take place, and Buckingham Palace has a room for projecting films. There are picture shows in the royal yacht too.

The late Queen Mary was a film fan – a fact which no doubt surprises people who thought of her only as a stiff old lady living in a closed world of antique furniture and petit point embroidery. She was an avid cinemagoer, and would sometimes slip quietly into a suburban picture house, accompanied only by a lady in waiting, to catch up with a film she had missed in the West End.

And Queen Mary's dry comments would have made entertaining film criticism.

Princess Margaret too is a cinema connoisseur (and, incidentally, this volatile royal lady has more than once been the subject of some of those sudden calls on my telephone from BBC News which I mentioned at the beginning of this chapter – notably one night in 1960 when there came unheralded the announcement of the engagement to Tony Armstrong-Jones, and then in 1976, sixteen years later, when on another night the story of the marriage break-up flared). Her Royal Highness has a taste for the arts that is above the Royal Family's average; and music and motion pictures are among her personal, not merely official, interests. And she knows the stars.

11

This was Churchill

The most illustrious film addict I ever came across – and in my job I came across him a very great deal through the years – was Winston Churchill. Watching films at home after dinner was one of his favourite relaxations, even during his crowded wartime years. He would sit in the Long Gallery at Chequers, the Buckinghamshire country house of British Prime Ministers, inviting Cabinet ministers, visiting statesmen, members of his staff and security guards to come and make an audience with him. He was not one for short documentaries. What he liked were full-length features, particularly the romantic dramas produced by his friend Alexander Korda. At Chartwell, his own home in West Kent, he had a downstairs dining-room turned into a cinema as soon as he went back to live in the house when the war ended in 1945. Cans of the latest pictures, and reels of old classics too, were regularly sent down from London to entertain the family and their guests and servants at week-ends. It was hard to keep up the supply.

I heard many an account of the film shows from people who were present at them. Churchill, with his cigar going, used to settle well down in an armchair in the front row near the screen. As the pictures whirred away he would from time to time make comments on the action and offer loud advice to the actors. He loved sentimental, melodramatic stuff, even souped-up travesties of history, 'costume epics', and popular musicals too. Simple pleasure in unsophisticated productions was manifest. The old film *Lady Hamilton* he saw over and over again with an enjoyment which seemed never to diminish, the beauty of Vivien Leigh attracting him as much as the battles of Lord

Nelson. The young singer Deanna Durbin was one of his favourite stars. He was much tickled by Chaplin's *The Great Dictator* and he relished *Gone with the Wind*. He liked all the musical numbers from *The Wizard of Oz* and often had records of them put on his gramophone. The records became scratchy from repeated use. But the song which took his fancy during the war was 'Run, Rabbit, Run', which for a time dethroned even his beloved Gilbert and Sullivan selections – though he was always liable to put a G and S disc on the radiogram when he had finished dictating in his study at two a.m., and would sing the numbers too.

He was no slave to television – for that matter, not really a good television performer either. He called TV 'a bloody harmful invention'. Words were his forte, so Sound radio was the medium which suited him. But he did listen to the wireless, to bulletins at any rate, and would refer to items in the News as something he had heard 'on the broadcast'.

One night during the war he heard an item in a late News on the BBC which he thought was wrong, so wrong that he was very cross and personally telephoned Broadcasting House to complain. The Duty Officer who answered the phone was terrified when a voice growled: 'This is the Prime Minister. Be so good as to connect me at once to the director in charge.' The Duty Officer scurried round, unavailingly: he could find nobody in high authority, and had to confess nervously to the irate caller that there was a senior officer in the building but he was 'asleep somewhere'. At this, our official had to spend the next few minutes receiving a series of blistering comments from the PM. At the end, when the poor man managed to get in an apology, he was surprised to hear the famous voice change its tone and say: 'May I thank you, whoever you may be, for having the patience and courtesy to listen to me.'

Churchill had enjoyed saying his piece. He liked an audience. He liked making a speech, making a broadcast. His radio scripts, with the carefully rehearsed 'impromptus' put in, bear witness to the trouble he took to prepare and practise them. Whether it was for the radio or the House of Commons, he was a model script writer and his English was just as good as the prose he wrote for the printed page. He had a prodigious memory and easily learned by heart the set speeches. Yet in Parliament he had every word on the paper in his hand – just in case he wanted to look down.

He was a natural broadcaster from the start, because he talked as his natural self, not putting on a special act for the microphone. But at first he felt a need for at least one visible hearer; and when he gave one of his early radio talks in 1934, a prophetic warning of the menace of Nazi Germany, he asked Stuart Hibberd, the BBC's chief announcer (in regulation dinner jacket in those days), to sit in front of him all the time in the studio. In Hibberd's words, 'he waved his arms about when emphasizing a point, exactly as he would do on a public platform. And he was excellent.'

And even more excellent during the war, when he made more broadcasts than at any other period of his life. I saw something of those famous performances, and the effect they had. His words were fighting weapons; the spirit they expressed in the direst times was the spirit of Britain. Here was this bulldog of a man, maverick and genius, brought suddenly, in 1940, from the political wilderness to be Britain's leader, and at once commanding universal attention and obedience. It is not an exaggeration to say that his broadcast phrases held the nation together; when he had finished speaking every man's back was a little straighter.

Every time he came on the air the whole country listened: for fifteen minutes men and women stopped whatever they were doing and sat in front of a radio set. Restaurants in the West End of London had empty tables galore when a Churchill speech was due; once he began speaking, public houses all over the land fell silent and no one ordered a drink, the customers all crowding near the bar radio and neither moving nor talking; normally busy telephone exchanges reported that they handled not a single call whilst the Prime Minister was on; and water boards' meters showed that consumption virtually stopped: nobody turned a tap, boiled a kettle or went to the lavatory.

Even if he had achieved nothing in the other eighty-five years of his extraordinarily active life, those five years of wartime leadership would have made him immortal. They were his own finest hours, and the broadcasts were peaks of his accomplishment.

I sat at his feet many times in the war years and in peacetime, and as a reporter watched him at close quarters in many situations at home and overseas. I wish I could recount how I interviewed him, but I never did. Nor did anybody else. He would never agree to journalistic interrogation in public: when he had something to say, he wrote it or he broadcast it or he spoke it to Parliament. He used to scowl and stride past when he saw waiting microphones and cameras. Once I very nearly thought I had him. Wearing his medals, he arrived at an Alamein Reunion shortly after the war, and when I asked him if he would say a few words for me, he hesitated and seemed to be considering the idea, but then shook his head and stumped away saying: 'I shall speak to the desert veterans from the stage. Put that on the broadcast.'

On quite another occasion, when he was returning from a visit to America I was on board his liner and persuaded him to give a rare impromptu press conference as we were coming up Southampton Water and preparing to disembark. My fellow correspondents were delighted that he had consented; and so was I – until he came into the room and announced: 'I will read to you a short statement and that will be all.' More disappointing still, he was unfolding his piece of paper when he saw my microphone ready on the table. He knew perfectly well what it was, but he poked it with his stick as though it were some poisonous reptile, and said: 'What is this device here? Let us dispense with it.'

I *almost* succeeded in getting Churchill interviews in 1958 when I was sent to the Riviera – first, to report his recovery from alarming pleurisy whilst he was staying at La Pausa, the villa of Emery Reves, his literary-agent friend (it was there I found Winston busy framing the words of the medical bulletins on himself); and, later, to cover the celebration of the Churchills' golden wedding in Monte Carlo. Each time, I was invited to enter the sunny garden where Sir Winston sat; each time I had the microphone in my hand; and each time he bade me put the thing away and hold a glass of Pol Roger instead.

A pity. I would love to have recorded even one Churchill sally – like the crack he made to Archbishop Temple when the German air raids were hitting Canterbury: 'You would be safe in your own cathedral crypt from any bombs, except perhaps from a direct hit by an armour-piercing missile. And if that should come, my dear Archbishop, it would best be regarded in the nature of a summons from on high.' In the BBC Sound Archives all his great speeches are enshrined, and can be re-heard in all their polished phrases and rolling splendour of delivery. But we have none of the instant aphorisms, the impish labels he gave to public people, the irreverent jokes uttered with that often-imitated sibilance and satirical stress.

One of his most cutting remarks – and we do have this one on the records – was that acid comment he made on seeing the controversial Graham Sutherland portrait of himself. I remember the occasion well because I was broadcasting it: the eightieth-birthday tribute to him. The combined Houses of Parliament, whose present this picture was, were massively assembled in Westminster Hall. Sir Winston sat hunched in his chair on the platform, chunky and pugnacious, and listened to the speeches without moving. When the curtains parted to reveal the painting on an easel behind him, he turned round, scowled briefly at it, and quickly swung back again. He plainly detested what the artist had done; and when presently he rose to make his speech he glared at the portrait once more and rumbled: 'A striking example of *modern* art. It certainly combines force and candour.' And he *spat* the word 'modern'. Undoubtedly the painting was brilliantly frank, a powerful artist's comment in oils, a picture of a strong old face with an element of cruelty in it, a head pillaged by the passage of the years. It is full of character, very striking indeed.

That portrait is one of the Churchill mysteries. It has disappeared. It has not been exhibited. It has never been seen from that day to this. Nor is it likely to appear: the family hate the work. It is not the man they wish posterity to behold.

But there are, in all conscience, plenty of portraits of him about. And statues. The statue I like best is the one I see most, the one at Westerham, not far from where I live. Westerham is near to Chartwell, which is now a Churchill museum and memorial in the care of the National Trust; and it is towards his old home that the larger-than-life bronze figure of the old statesman is looking as he reclines there on the Westerham village green. The figure is dressed in his rompers, in one of the favourite baggy open-necked boiler-suits, and is very natural and relaxed and lifelike, contrasting with the other statue on the green – Westerham-born General Wolfe of Quebec, who stands in heroic pose, waving a sword on high and wearing a dressy cocked hat. It is fitting that those two men should be neighbours in effigy. Two centuries of time separated their lives but they were fellow spirits, both of them chivalrous English soldiers and great servants of an Empire.

Winston Churchill liked wearing those blue rompers so much that he had corduroy velvet versions of them made for evening wear at dinner. In the war years the garments were known as Winnie's siren suits, easy to slip on when the air-raid sirens went. But in fact they dated from the twenties and thirties when Churchill wore such things as working overalls whilst he indulged his happy pastime of bricklaying at Chartwell.

Pictures of life in that country house which was the family home for four decades were wonderfully evoked for me one day when I had a long interview with Sir Winston's daughter Mary, Lady Soames, who recalled especially the years before the Second World War when her father was something of a political outcast and spent much of his time at home with the family, not sitting back and moping but busying himself enormously both inside and outside the house. 'Life certainly had its ups and downs,' said Lady Soames, 'and sometimes we were economizing and living in just one small wing. But, with my father there, life never seemed mingy. There was always enchanting talk and diverting things to be done. He wrote and he painted and he brooded. But he constructed too – loved to be busy with his hands. He had an absolute passion for construction: walls, cottages, dams, swimming pools – he made them all, with the utmost enthusiasm. Never idle for a moment. And I believe that at Chartwell he never knew a day's boredom or unhappiness. Once he said: "Every day away from here is a day wasted."

After his epic years as wartime leader (siren-suited even at the microphone), Winston Churchill was Premier again a decade later – and in Westminster Hall on his 80th birthday made wry comment on the candid portrait given him by Parliament (page 143)

People camping out in bitter cold to see the Churchill funeral in 1965 recalled scenes at other State pageants, very different events but in similar weather. In this picture, crowds wait for Princess Elizabeth's wedding procession in 1947 (pages 81–85)

Public figures were pall-bearers at the funeral of the statesman they had served. In front of St Paul's after the Churchill service (from the left): Attlee; Eden; Slim; Portal; Bridges, Normanbrook (former Secretaries to the Cabinet); Menzies; Templer; Macmillan (page 153)

The body of Sir Winston in its heavy coffin is borne down the
steps of the Cathedral —

– and from the Thames to Festival Pier. Lady Churchill and her
son Randolph follow immediately behind the coffin. Leading
the party walks the Earl Marshal, 'lone and imperious in plumed
hat . . .' (pages 151–154)

Royal Wedding 1973. The Abbey scene on which I looked down.
Princess Anne hands her bouquet to the tiny Lady Sarah
Armstrong-Jones, whilst a kilted Prince Edward guards her
train. The Royal Family watch from the sanctuary. Prince
Rainier and Princess Grace of Monaco are in the front row next
to the steps (page 160)

'And it was to Chartwell, of course, that there came, in the years of gathering storm before the war, his friends, the political confederates, the shadowy messengers from Europe who would talk to him far into the night, telling grim stories from Germany and all bearing witness that time was running short.'

Then, through the great man's days in office – his days of glory – he would always go to Chartwell from London whenever he could, even for a few hours. And the house, with its solace, was waiting for him, when times of sadness and defeat came. In Lady Soames' words: 'I shall always remember the evening when he came back home to us after he had been to Buckingham Palace to submit his resignation to the Queen. He went straight upstairs to the study and just sat there, looking at the familiar things in the place where he had worked at his book writing for so long. All of us in the house were a bit subdued and overcome. Meanwhile a little crowd of people had come up the lane and were standing quietly, just sympathizing, outside the gates; and somebody asked him if he could send a message to them. He stirred himself and went to the door where the people had come; and he spoke just half a dozen words, simply and very quietly: "It's always nice to come home".'

There are other pictures of the Chartwell life and the Winston Churchill enthusiasms. The passion for long and steaming-hot baths twice a day in between meals and naps and hours of padding up and down dictating his memoirs and histories. His flow of masterful talk would continue from the tub, for he went on dictating in the bath – to a secretary hovering with notebook just outside the bathroom door.

I used to talk with old Henry Whitbread, an ex-company sergeant-major who lived in Westerham and taught Mr Churchill how to lay bricks and worked alongside him in that lovely Kentish garden with its marvellous views across the Weald. He told me of talks they used to have as they plied mortar and trowel, the great man laying his bricks with gusto and speed (Whitbread used to go back at night sometimes to make a few quiet corrections to his fellow worker's line and setting): 'He was very proud of his construction work, so tickled at the start that he joined the bricklayers' union. He had a union card too. Of course they'd never had a member who worked in a Homburg hat and had a whisky glass beside him and mixed cigar ash with the mortar. They'd never had a member with his politics!'

Whitbread himself was an out-and-out socialist, who expressed his views without fear to his Tory fellow worker at ·Chartwell. And Winston used to say: 'He's a Labourite, but quite nice. Taught me about life as well as bricks.'

I was once asked by an American broadcasting organization to record for them a four-minute 'profile' of Winston Churchill. I turned the request down: there was too much for any four minutes, too many talents, too many contradictions, too many years. It was like being asked to paint a miniature of a colossus. And yet of course during his life we broadcast about him endlessly, for he was not ordinary and was larger than life. It didn't matter that his last few years were anticlimax, his figure not seen, his voice stilled as he sat at home waiting inscrutably for the end.

When the end did at last come, at the age of ninety, the salute that was given was an amazing spectacle – and the broadcasting of it a story in itself. If I live to be a hundred there will still be in my mind the Day of the Funeral.

12

A Last Salute

One afternoon early in January 1965 I was in my BBC office, entrapped in the chores of Reporting Organizer, when word came that the old warrior was dying. We had been prepared for such news for a long time; and now many people had to be alerted for action. Such was Winston Churchill's eminence that special programmes about him, and long news obituaries, had been ready, revised and revised, for very many years. Preparations to cover the inevitable obsequies too. In the last, ten years he had suffered strokes and falls and various ailments, had recovered from them all, but then had gradually succumbed to the quiet creep of senility. Now he was at his London home, Hyde Park Gate, in a coma. On 15 January news was released that he had suffered another stroke four days before, and doctors' bulletins showed that he was sinking.

It was necessary for certain moves to be made. In Whitehall, stand-by orders were given. Private planning meetings were called at the BBC, at Television Centre, at the College of Arms and at the headquarters of the army's London District at the Horse Guards. For at the Queen's wish, intimated long before, there would be a state funeral. Churchill was to be buried like a king.

Bulky files were brought out in our own Broadcasting House as well as at the Earl Marshal's office in the Heralds' College in Queen Victoria Street, where the Duke of Norfolk presided over those antiquaries and experts on ceremonial who bear such names as Clarenceux, Portcullis and Bluemantle. The files, ours and the heralds', bore the code name 'Operation Hope Not'. A funeral plan had existed for the past decade and in the last five years had been brought to detail. (Long before, Winston himself had known that there would be a memorial service, and had said what music he would like.) Such preparations were necessary: the death of this great person would come one day, and when it did it would set in train a vast piece of ceremonial which could not be created overnight. It was always private and precautionary planning, of course. Even now, ominous though Lord Moran's medical reports were, the files might even yet again be going back into their locked cupboards – they had been out so often, and so often there had been remarkable recovery by the old man.

But on Sunday morning, 24 January, Winston Churchill died, ninety years old. Long though the event had been expected, the announcement had great impact. Messages of tribute came from all over the world; and the media gave fullest treatment to the statesman's life and work. Saturday the 30th was fixed for the funeral; and churchmen and soldiers, government ministries and Scotland Yard, railway chiefs and River Thames authorities, book printers and broadcasters – they all addressed themselves to the final days, to the Last Salute.

And while the pageant of remembrance and thanksgiving for an exceptional life was being mounted, and while for five days Sir Winston's body lay in panoplied state in Westminster Hall, I remembered the man and his times. I had to remember – professionally. I was called to give talks about him, for he had bulked large in my own life as a reporter.

There was much to remember. The 'unemployed' twenties and thirties when he built his walls and ponds at Chartwell; the 1940 call to Downing Street when the kingdom was in mortal peril; his relish of supreme command – the impatience and inconsiderateness and mulishness too, the way he gave hell to his staffs night and day; the schoolboyish sense of humour as well as the scintillating language; the cruel blow dealt to him when the voters threw him out of office just when he had won the war; the stateliness and courtesy of the later years, the surges of magnanimity and generosity which swept over the rocks of his harshness – all this had to be recalled, recalled to a new, denigrating generation which did not perhaps know or care that but for this old man and his patriot-ism and word power we might well have been, all of us and to this day, in thrall to jackboot monsters.

Such were the memories as we got ready for the funeral rite which was to make the nation stand to attention – and radio and television to pull out all the stops in the most complex OB programme in BBC history, heard and seen by a world audience greater than ever before.

The man who had been master of Britain's ceremonies for decades was in charge of the funeral: the sixteenth Duke of Norfolk, hereditary Earl Marshal of England. His heralds had looked into their old books, studying major funerals of the past – Marlborough, Pitt, Nelson, Canning, the Iron Duke, Gladstone – and it was the great Duke of Wellington's funeral which formed the pattern on which he based the Churchill ceremony. To prepare for it, hundreds of men were involved in work night and day. The Earl Marshal personally superin-tended every detail with the gruff efficiency and precise sense of occasion which had characterized his faultless presenting of coronations and other days of pomp through four decades of the century. Quiet and naturally shy, but confident and competent, Bernard Norfolk sat at his desk and master-minded the whole thing. He had rehearsed secretly for ten years.

On the day before the funeral he was out inspecting every point of the route. Long before dawn, he led the procession of troops and carriages and horses on its final rehearsal through the streets of London to St Paul's Cathedral, where the service was to be held. The rehearsal morning was almost as un-forgettable as The Day itself. It was perishingly cold; the wind cut our faces like a knife and made us long for shelter and hot breakfast. But there was the Duke of Norfolk, impervious to such things as weather, in dark overcoat and bowler hat, self-contained and laconic, hopping in and out of cars, telling soldiers and civilians what to do, and pacing down the middle of empty streets with his staff trailing behind him.

With the Earl Marshal's group was the diligent Richard Dimbleby, television's unrivalled commentator, now at the peak of his career, himself with attendants: secretary and producer, note-takers and timekeepers. (The Duke made his own notes; his own clip-board was under his arm, his own stopwatch in his hand.)

Dimbleby, I remember, was watching and talking and scribbling in a notebook all the morning with his customary thoroughness, though in fact he was feeling unwell (and was to die himself, at fifty-two, before the year was out). No stranger would have guessed – for he had more energy and more cheerfulness than any of us – that a dread disease was now painfully gripping his back. He never suggested infirmity. Nor had he any notion of giving in; a standby commentator's presence was only a routine precaution – though, as a matter of fact, that morning's stand-by was another very conscientious man. He was Tom Fleming, the sound Scottish actor who in the last ten years has become a well-known broadcasting voice, often taking the old Dimbleby place at the microphone at state ceremonies. In January 1965 he was still 'looking and learning,' dour and self-effacing in a long Inverness cape.

The rehearsal was an eerie business. We moved in the early darkness through city streets which most of us had previously seen only as daytime canyons clogged with vehicles and jostling pedestrians, but which were now hollow and nearly empty, echoing only with the hoofbeats of the cavalry and the crunch of carriage wheels. London seemed weird and quite unfamiliar. We saw the huge silent buildings in a kind of stately nakedness under the night lights, as though we were seeing them for the first time.

Next morning, Saturday, all was different – except the weather, which was arctic. The Earl Marshal felt called upon to utter a typical dry comment: 'Very reasonable day. Might have been four inches of snow.' The processional route from Westminster to St Paul's and through the City to Tower Pier was thickly lined with people from an early hour, cold or no cold. Blue-faced, cherry-nosed and weeping with more than emotion, they stood with blankets round shoulders and old newspapers round feet, beating their hands together and taking nips from flasks. They had come to see the passing of a great captain of much of their own history. But these were not mournful people. This was not a day of lamentation for a sudden tragedy:

Winnie had enjoyed a wonderful long innings; it did not matter that in the last few years he had rarely been seen and had almost ceased to exist as far as they were concerned. For the patient thousands, being there on the pavements was an act of cheerful remembrance and thanksgiving. A hundred Churchill jokes were bandied about, with rough imitations of his voice.

But people were solemn when at last the slow cortège came, along streets lined by troops, streets that were complete and safe on this day but had so often been gap-toothed and choked with bomb smoke and air-raid debris in the wartime when the man now in the coffin gave a lion's roar of courage and defiance. No jokes in the crowd now, but just looking; looking at the soldiers marching with guns reversed, the horsemen, the carriages, the famous people riding and walking as chief mourners, the ten bands, the unshakeable Norfolk, lone and imperious in plumed hat, and then the gun carriage drawn by a hundred and fifty sailors. On this carriage lay the coffin draped in a Union Jack and with the dead man's Garter insignia on top of it.

And so to the Cathedral. Here the coffin rested in splendour beneath the dome, and all around it the congregation was a mosaic of three thousand faces. Such a congregation! The entire Churchill clan, the Queen and all the Royal Family, every imaginable famous public figure of the United Kingdom and the overseas countries of the Commonwealth, seventeen prime ministers, and Heads of State and representatives of a hundred foreign lands. De Gaulle was there, and Eisenhower; reigning sovereigns of Norway and Denmark, Holland and Belgium.

Unaccountably, I thought, no President Johnson, and not even his *Vice*-President. Chief Justice Earl Warren was the best that the USA could do to honour the memory of Winston Churchill, America's only honorary citizen and greatest friend.

Also surprisingly, Montgomery was not present. The Field Marshal, then seventy-seven, who had become very close to Winston in the later years, was in South Africa and, though sorrowing, he stayed there. He sent a message which Winston would have appreciated: 'No use going to the funeral of an old friend and finishing dead yourself.'

Many of Churchill's old comrades, and old adversaries, did turn up, however, and suffered the weather. Fragile old men, some of them. Two of them came without motor-car or carriage: President Shazar of Israel, seventy-six, and old David Ben-Gurion, seventy-eight, walked on that bitter day to and from St Paul's. It was the Jewish Sabbath and they could not ride.

The man who drew the sympathy of millions was the eighty-two-years-old Labour leader Earl Attlee, who, invited to be one of the twelve eminent pallbearers, deliberately hazarded his health and came to give this last service to his wartime chief and old opponent.

Deathly pale and tottering as he waited on the steps outside the Cathedral after the service, he was lent a helping arm by a giant of a Guards officer and led to a little kitchen chair which was brought out for him. On this he sat, hunched over his stick, eyes screwed up against the wind, until he was helped down to his car, a sombre figure between the stationary lines of heralds in their bright medieval tabards. We were glad to see him safely inside the limousine. Clem Attlee had given even more cause for alarm before the service when he had been walking up the steps immediately in front of the coffin as it was being carried, steeply tilted, up the steps to the church's West Door.

The coffin was cruelly heavy. Made of thick oak and lined with lead, it weighed a quarter of a ton, a terrible burden even for the eight young bareheaded Grenadiers who formed the bearer party, and a very difficult one to carry on the shoulders when mounting steps. A continuous, smooth walk, with every man in step, was essential – and it was that rhythm which was precariously broken when Lord Attlee faltered and caused the bearers momentarily to stop. For an anxious moment the whole mass of their precious load was jolted on to the back men; there was a perceptible wavering as the coffin slipped – and a swift intake of breath from watchers who saw danger of disaster. But the soldiers just managed to hold firm; they steadied; and the old man in front of them righted himself and walked up and on. The body was borne safely into the waiting cathedral.

Those eight Guardsmen drew everybody's eyes. No doubt the attitude was a prescribed part of bearing a dead-weight on the shoulders at a funeral, but the sight of those fresh-faced British soldiers with their cheeks pressed against Winston Churchill's coffin was hauntingly poignant.

To see the other pallbearers whom Lord Attlee joined was to recall our embattled yesterdays: two ranks of greatness walking down the cathedral aisle – Mountbatten, Macmillan, Menzies, Eden, Alexander, Slim, Templer, Portal, Ismay, Bridges and Normanbrook. All of them Churchill's captains and colleagues.

The service could not have been more pertinent: 'To Be a Pilgrim', resoundingly sung . . . 'Who would true valour see, let him come hither'. And the Battle Hymn of the Republic . . . 'Let us die to make men free'. At the close, we looked down on the coffin wrapped in its bright banner being carried out slowly along a blue carpet that stretched to the doors, and it did not steer an exact geometrically straight line but rather seemed to weave as though floating along a blue river. We were singing 'O God our Help in Ages Past' and there came the words: 'Time, like an ever rolling stream, bears all its sons away'. And there he was, on his last journey, being borne away on that stream of blue. It was all almost unbearably apt.

The day's pageantry was broadcast to the world, five hours of continuous transmission. It went by Eurovision, by satellite Telstar, by videotape and film to four hundred million watchers. Eighty TV cameras were deployed. One cameraman, stationed high above the dome of the cathedral for all those hours, had to be thawed out and carefully unbent when he was brought down ice-rimed and half dead.

After St Paul's the coffin was taken in gun-carriage procession once more, down Cannon Street and Eastcheap to the Tower of London. By the time it reached there, I was in position at a commentary point high on an open stand between the battlements of the fortress and the embankment of the Thames. My job was to describe the last journey, by water. It was colder than ever there beside the grey, whipped-up waves of the river. I wore a pair of pyjamas beneath my day clothes, two overcoats and an oilskin on top. The BBC, exceptionally, had provided tots of spirits and pots of coffee to keep its servants going. And yet my teeth chattered as I talked.

Sixty pipers played a lament as the stoic bearers took the body to the pontoon of Tower Pier (the men rested their burden on a side wall for a few seconds just before the river's edge, when they were briefly out of sight of cameras and onlookers: their load was back-breaking, and had almost slipped from their grasp a second time when they were coming *down* the steps of St Paul's). From the Tower a Port of London Authority launch took the coffin up river to the Festival Hall pier and so to Waterloo station, whilst guns boomed and fighters of the RAF swooped low in salute. There was also a surprise piece of riverside theatre: as the launch went past the wharves of the South Bank every jib of the line of giant cranes dipped in dramatic unison – the most unusual gesture of the day.

The day ended with the transporting of the body by train to Oxfordshire and a private burial at Bladon village, near to the palace of Blenheim where Sir Winston was born. He once had thought he would like to be buried at Blenheim; then in his old age decided it must be Chartwell; but after a visit to Bladon with Lady Churchill he changed his mind yet again. Walking round the churchyard there in the rain one day, hunched in a fat teddy-bear coat, he tapped an empty plot of ground with his stick. 'This is my place, here,' he said. So not for him the stony splendours of Westminster Abbey as a final resting place – the story is that he declared there were too many people lying there already whom he didn't like – but the remote simplicity of an English countryside. He was buried where the Spencer-Churchills are together as a family in death, near the graves of his parents, Lord Randolph and the lovely Jennie, Lady Randolph.

From the London streets, on that funeral day, I went back to Broadcasting House. I had one more task: to narrate for radio an edited version of the commentaries. That done, I was leaving the building, very tired indeed, when the reception desk in the front hall called: 'Stop please, Mr Talbot, the News Room are after you. It's very important.'

I had to turn back. But there *couldn't* be another Big Story on this same day, I thought. There could! A flash on the news agency tapes had just come in: 'Duke of Gloucester in car smash. First reports say feared dead on return from Churchill funeral.' So it was panic stations; and I spent the next two hours telephoning and writing and talking on the air, a long heavy day becoming longer and heavier. But the news was not as bad as it had seemed. The Duke and Duchess, the ill-fated royal Gloucesters, driving home to Barnwell Manor, had somersaulted off the A 1 and their car finished on its roof in a potato field. Both sustained some injury, though were by no means dead. But it was a scare; it was a news story – and a tricky business to get the facts right.

First reports of mishaps are sometimes very exaggerated and misleading. Many instances come to mind. A comparatively recent one occurred on the night of 20 March 1974, when the flash was: 'Princess Anne shot by killer gunman in Mall.' I was caught in the news-frenzy of that night too, though by then I had left the BBC's staff and was called in as a freelance. I spoke five news-comments within an hour, including one into a broadcasting network in Australia, 'live' from my telephone at home. In the chaos and confusion precipitated by the hold-up of the royal car, it took a long time for the detail to emerge and the picture to focus. The Princess was not in fact injured. Other people were shot, grievously hurt, but Her Royal Highness and her husband Captain Mark Phillips emerged unharmed from a mad attempt at kidnapping within a few yards of the Buckingham Palace gates. An alarming occurrence in a London even then fast becoming a cockpit of street violence.

The Princess showed something of her mother's coolness in hazard that evening. Very soon after the shootings, she was inside the Palace and on the telephone giving a succinct account of the hold-up to her parents on the other side of the world – for the Queen and Prince Philip were on a visit to Indonesia and were awakened at four a.m. local time to receive the first-hand story of their daughter's escape.

That attack in the Mall came only four months after Princess Anne had become Mrs Mark Phillips, and even before it happened the young couple were still very much 'in the news'. Their wedding had been another commentators' field-day. Myself, I have never experienced anything quite like it. I had the biggest single work-load of my whole broadcasting life – even though I was not, for once, talking to the world.

13

Backstage in the Abbey

The day was Wednesday, 14 November 1973. The place: Westminster, naturally. On the face of it, the whole thing might have been for me just another broadcast in the long string of OBs from the old Abbey, all routine and *déjà vu*. Especially as this Princess Anne wedding was a repeat of the Queen's wedding, on another November day twenty-six years earlier, in that its setting was again a wintry Britain in economic crisis – indeed, what with the threat of petrol rationing and all, things were even worse than in 1947. And especially as this marriage too was getting the same sort of welcome, hailed as a brief kindly light amid the encircling gloom.

But in fact the Princess Anne happenings were not the mixture as before.

For one thing, after several years of quiescence, popular interest in the Royal Family was bubbling sentimentally to a new peak at the spectacle of the Present Generation Girl choosing a real outsider, a nice but new sort of commoner to be brought out of the blue and into the chosen circle. True, Princess Margaret had married a professional photographer from a studio in a disused ironmonger's shop in Pimlico, but this time it was the Sovereign's swinging daughter marrying one of her horse-jumping rivals – and there had been months of seeing the pair of them on the telly, months of titillating 'just-good-friends' denials that there was any Mark Phillips romance at all.

For another thing, on this wedding day I myself was, professionally, wearing a new hat, not a BBC one. After thirty-two years, I had retired from the official ranks of the Corporation staff and was doing a day's work for 'the other side', the then-raw but now very professional LBC.

Commerical radio was starting in Britain, and its first station, London Broadcasting Company, anxious to make an early impact and do the wedding in style in daring competition with the Old Firm, the BBC, jumped in and for once seduced me from Auntie's employ. They did so before they ever went on the air at all: they didn't start broadcasting until five weeks before the wedding date. I was engaged by special contract – 'no advertising breaks whilst you are on the air' – to cover the wedding exclusively for LBC and speak their main commentary. (At first, after so many long years in the fold of public service broadcasting, I was a little nervous at the prospect of working, however temporarily, for the profit-minded Other Side, and feared that somehow or other I might find my descriptions interrupted by Here's-a-word-from-our-Sponsor routines; but I need not have worried: the pledge that commercial breaks would be suspended was scrupulously kept when the time came. The tone of the presentation on that day was positively stately – 'Just like the Beeb,' someone said afterwards.)

Although I was hired 'for the day', in fact I had to work for a long time beforehand: you cannot do too much 'prep' for a set-piece OB. There is always a mass of background to absorb, and in this case the event had a lot of effects long before it took place.

As soon as it was announced that the wedding was to come, an extraordinary business ballyhoo began. Swiftly on to the market came Anne-and-Mark goblets, commemorative mugs, matchboxes, badges, wall plaques, inscribed ashtrays and plaster busts. Special statuettes of the pair on horseback were offered; the faces of bride and groom reproduced on pieces of gold and crystal and fine china came at nearly a thousand pounds a time; a Royal Wedding ale was brewed. And the souvenirs sold well: it was a six million pounds' bonanza. Never had there been such a commercial spin-off.

It is unlikely that the Royal Family were entranced by the extravagances of the wedding industry, though the better mementoes were 'approved'. There is no doubt that the

Princess herself would have liked a quieter wedding, perhaps a country church one. But Her Royal Highness had no chance, independent and strong-willed though she is: royal weddings are held in great churches in London, and Westminster Abbey, the royal peculiar, has long been their scene. That is tradition, and the Queen is for tradition. So we had the Princess dutifully attending preliminary meetings and rehearsals at the Abbey, and agreeing to maternal and musicianly suggestions about what the hymns and anthems should be. 'Crimond' was on the programme, of course, that was as certain as sunrise: the metrical Scottish paraphrase of the Twenty-Third Psalm, 'The Lord's My Shepherd', had become almost inseparable from any big choral service in which the Queen had a say. And, as Her Majesty loves descants, Dr Douglas Guest, the Abbey's Master of Music, wrote some specially for the day.

Everybody concerned said that Anne and her young dragoon – she was twenty-three and he was twenty-five – were very good about discussing the ceremony in advance with the Abbey authorities. The Princess followed her mother's taste and the organist's advice over the music. As to Captain Phillips, he swam with the tide until it came to deciding what should be played as they walked out through choir and nave at the end of the service. He struck out for himself then, and asked for his regimental march. At this request there was a shaking of heads, for, his regiment being the Queen's Dragoon Guards, the tune would be Johann Strauss's 'Radetzsky', a fast trot. No, said the bride, it's not suitable. I couldn't keep up that pace, certainly not in wedding shoes. So it was decided that, instead, the procession would walk out to a well-tried piece, Widor's Toccata in F Major. But as the bridegroom still wanted to hear his Strauss, it was agreed that there would be a touch of the lively 'Radetzsky' when the newly-wedded pair had got to the West Door. And so it was. On the day, the Captain did hear his music as they waited for their coach under the awning by the door. The Queen and the Royal Family were coming down the nave at that moment, but the brisk sound caused no disarray to *them*: it would take more than a cavalry clip to make the Queen hurry through Westminster

Abbey. (As a matter of musical interest, Dr Guest, at the planning stage when the music was being debated, had experimented with the tempo of the march, playing it slowly so that it might perhaps be suitable after all for a stately exit; but it sounded like a polka.)

During the preparations there had also been some concern over the television cameras, many of which were to be stationed in the Abbey with the full blessing of the bride's family and the Dean. But even in 1973 a certain royal nervousness over intrusive photography was manifest, and the go-ahead to TV had one proviso: no cameras whatever were to be placed east of the couple, between them and the altar as they stood at the sanctuary steps – no lenses directed at their faces as they exchanged their solemn vows. For certain memories lingered at Buckingham Palace, memories of the film pictures of a wedding in Monte Carlo seventeen years before when the beautiful Miss Kelly of Hollywood – in her Metro-Goldwyn-Mayer dress – became Her Serene Highness Princess Grace of Monaco. At that ceremony cameras and microphones were poking about all over the place during the nuptial mass, even behind the altar; and the film had shown the inelegant spectacle of guests, as they waited to leave, scrambling to pluck and pocket sprigs of bridal lilac and lilies as souvenirs. Westminster must have none of that. (Nor did it have. Everything was decent, dignified and happy and lovely to see. And, incidentally, Princess Grace, with her husband Prince Rainier, was in the Westminster congregation. She wore flowing white, looked gorgeous and walked like a queen. Every head turned as she came in. Amazing Grace.)

When 14 November dawned, indeed several hours before first light, London was exceptionally astir. Thousands of enthusiasts who had slept out all night on freezing cold pavements were emerging from blankets and sleeping bags and keeping life going by sending gulps of whisky and thermos-coffee coursing through their veins. Boy Scouts in well-washed khaki were setting out in the dark from suburban homes to sell programmes along the route. Policemen were being dropped by the coachload at their deploying points. Ambulance-men were checking their stretchers and first-aid satchels. The

Royal Mews was alive – and kicking. At the Household Cavalry barracks in Knightsbridge, troopers of the Life Guards and the Blues and Royals were polishing their chargers and themselves: tunics, pantaloons, jackboots and cuirasses had to be 'as new' this morning. Eager-beaver Press photographers – delighted that the dawn was showing a fine sunny day in prospect – were arriving at street-corner Press stands to get good places. Yeomen of the Guard and Gentlemen at Arms, the royal bodyguards, were flexing their old muscles and preening their ruffs and swan's-feather helmets. Ushers who had been chosen to guide the Abbey guests to their places were up and about and getting their wives to give a final brush to morning coats and uniforms. An inspection of the choir-boys in Dean's Yard would soon be making sure that surplices were clean and larynges clear. While inside the church itself security guards were on the prowl.

And the commentators? If *they* weren't 'ready for the off' by now, they might as well not try. But of course they were. This was the sort of operation the BBC had been carrying out for forty years, a whopping OB of which there had been plenty of notice. This wedding's coverage had been planned for months by experts, researched and rehearsed for weeks by experienced speakers.

But this time, such a familiar, leisurely run-up was not for me. No weeks of prayer and meditation, no coddling, no gangs of helpers and teams of technicians all long-prepared. This time I was the servant of the steely little newcomer, commercial sound-broadcasting – of the LBC station first in the field, which was living from day to day. So busy were the newly-recruited band of young LBC workers in getting their pioneer transmissions on the air at all, so understandably absorbed with their teething troubles, that they had no time for long meetings about the details of 14 November, big prestige operation though they intended their wedding coverage to be. And I began to get anxious. However, as the day drew terrify-ingly near and realization grew of the size and complication of the coverage to which they were committed, overworked and sleepless seniors of LBC perforce addressed themselves with vigour and enthusiasm to the sheets of outline plans and

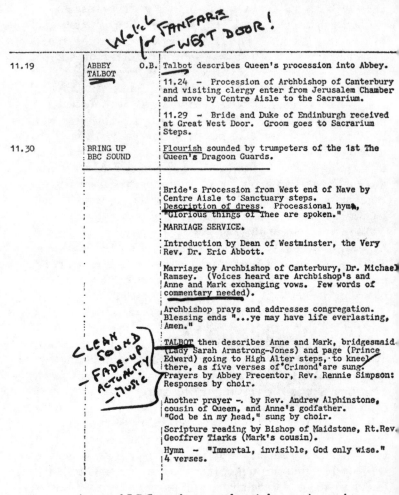

A page of LBC cue-sheets — and reminder notes! — used during my commentary on Princess Anne's wedding at Westminster.

service timings which I had tried to work out for them. And everybody rose to the occasion.

I was to be the station's anchorman, linking the whole day's coverage from my commentary point inside the Abbey, but the scenes in the processional streets outside were to be reported, also 'live', by a team of young broadcasters, some of them inevitably prentice hands (and who, on the day, acquitted themselves with honour). These new colleagues were now gathered together, briefed, and issued with brand-new two-way wireless sets so that, it was hoped, they would be heard describing all the passing sights and surrounding jollifications direct from their appointed positions among the crowds. Lines were also laid and microphone points installed in front of Buckingham Palace and facing the West Front of the Abbey. Last-minute practices were attended, night conferences held, a little van was brought into Dean's Yard and crammed with technical gear so that it could be the operational control point, and inside the Abbey a special observation nest for me was built and furnished.

My perch was a small, glass-walled commentary box jutting out into mid-air from the triforium above the south-east corner of the choir, a spur so suspended in space (though, happily, strongly guyed and counterweighted) that the young lady who was to be my message-feeding assistant in this eyrie during the broadcast shuddered and shut her eyes when she first saw the thing, and declared that nothing would induce her to set foot on such a frightening projection, at any rate not without a stiff gin and a seat-belt. When I first climbed up and got into the box it was, I must admit, quite breathtaking to sit there – as though on the far end of an aircraft wing thrust out into nothingness. But a superb vantage point. I had never had such a view in all the BBC years of being in the Abbey. Sanctuary and choir, lantern and transepts, organ loft and nave, even the private chapel of Edward the Confessor where they would sign the marriage registers – my view commanded all these.

I could see everything, but nobody could see me. And so – instead of sweating in my formal clothes under the blazing TV floodlights which were so near to me up there – I was able to broadcast comfortably in my shirtsleeves, with morning coat shed, braces down, tie off and shoes undone.

As to fear of my high perch, that vanished the moment broadcasting began. The scene on the day was so absorbing that I had no moment to be scared of the abyss below me. I was in the Abbey before seven a.m. and, once our programme began I talked, with not many breaks, from eight until one. We broadcast the gathering of the crowds, the sweeping of the streets, the assembling of the troops, the hilarities of the spectators, the bands, the cheers, the carriages and cavalry escorts, and of course every activity in the Abbey from the moment I got there long before the service started. I had to link the outside reports every time I heard the words 'Now back to Godfrey Talbot' in my earphones, as well as describe the scene below me. It was a marvellous job to be tackling. There was a lot to tell.

No other wedding had produced such strange preliminaries. Long before the service began, long before the congregation were admitted, long before even the first stirrings of vergers and ushers and last-minute cleaners of carpets, I watched a security sweep down below. The Abbey had been closed to the public for nine days and guards had been sleeping inside it; every door had been manned and nobody admitted except on production of a series of special passes, for bomb scares and threats of wedding day terrorism had created an atmosphere of acute anxiety and a time of heavy duty for the forces responsible for public order and the protection of VIPs. So now, on the morning itself, there were police and firemen moving through the Abbey; plain-clothes detectives and Special Branch officers stalked the precincts; bomb detection experts lay in reserve; and – it was almost difficult to believe one's eyes – here came a string of animals padding along the aisle: tracker dogs! The Alsatians and their handlers went searching along every row of seats, sniffing for explosives, watching for suspicious objects.

Nothing evil was found (indeed, the whole day passed off 'without incident'), and men and animals disappeared into unseen corners and galleries before the public came and the TV cameras brought the inside of the church into world view.

It was, as ever, a lovely service to see and to hear. Once the congregation had assembled, the central figures had come and the marriage ceremony had begun, television pictures told the story and the music and the sound of the old Prayer Book words took over. And my own duty as a commentator on radio was to supplement what was naturally heard, to identify the voices, briefly explain the ritual movements, describe the scene, but always to let the sound effects speak for themselves. The chief anxiety on these occasions is lest you do not watch the musicians and get caught in mid-sentence by a blast of trumpets, lest your own talk overlaps the words of Archbishop or Dean, and lest you commit the sin of chattering during a beautiful anthem which everyone wishes to hear uninterrupted.

What *is* required, if it is the millions who are *not* in front of the television set whom you are serving, is a word picture of the chief actors. Accordingly, I did my best to sketch Captain Phillips, a perfect toy soldier in tight scarlet tunic and blue overalls and Wellington boots, and to say how well he managed to avoid getting his swan-necked spurs caught on the sacrarium steps; to describe Princess Anne in her white silk gown and great Elizabethan sleeves, and to report that she and her father were chatting with the greatest informality as they walked in; to give an impression of the Queen's fitted coat of sapphire blue and the hat that was all lacey snood; to convey as well as possible the pretty picture which Princess Margaret's nine-year-old daughter made: Lady Sarah Armstrong Jones in a pinafore dress and Juliet cap. And – just as eye-catching as the ladies – the other bridal attendant, also aged nine, little brother Prince Edward in white silk shirt and Royal Stewart kilt.

The two thousand people in the congregation were not, this time, the usual mixture of top brass and titled officials. True, there were a few politicians and generals and a knight or two; but they had been invited as people, as individuals rather than holders of offices. It was not an occasion when you *had* to invite the usual crowd from government and Foreign Office lists; and Anne and Mark had sent invitations to people they knew and liked and wanted to be present. And so it was a fascinating and unusual cross-section of people that I looked down on: the bride's personal friends, school companions, sportsmen, horsey people, Palace servants. There sat Mrs Phillips' daily-help lady from Great Somerford village, the local saddler and blacksmith and their wives; there was Jackie Stewart from the world of racing cars, tennis's Dan Maskell and the Turf's own Fred Winter; and riding folk like Richard Meade and Alison Oliver. There was Mabel Anderson, who was Princess Anne's nanny, sitting up at the front with famous field marshals and a prince or two. Not a single ambassador was present, not unless he was a personal friend (At this breezy ignoring of official lists many a diplomat's wife was livid).

On the surface, nevertheless, the wedding was a glittering pageant (and the general public would have been disappointed if it had not been). Some of my more cynical friends – to whom tradition is a dirty word – muttered: 'Just a dress parade – pure operetta!' Some viewed it as a piece of theatre, a concert – and I recall one critical bystander (admittedly a sort of boffin, a perfectionist sound-engineer) who opened his mouth just once to say: 'The Arch has a touch of the tremolos.' But I think the experience of the morning was something simple and pure and pleasing to most people. The impression this particular Abbey service gave, for all the processional grandeur, was of an event which was rather unsophisticated and unaffectedly blithe. It gave out the sort of joy you get at a village wedding when everybody knows everybody else and the whole lot are enjoying themselves. Like the congregation, the bridal party seemed to be relaxed and pleased to be there. The sixteenth-century words of the marriage rite sounded lovely. The Royal Family were *people*, not ritual figures. I believe even that dedicated swiper at the monarchy, Willie Hamilton, had he been there, might have had a tiny bit of a lump in his throat.

That cosy family feeling and informal impression was all the more remarkable *because* the wedding of course never ceased to be Grand Spectacle. It had all the patina of a state ceremony ordered by the Sovereign. But in fact, as I say, it was not strictly such a ceremony. It had been organized by a band of men who, though largely unsung, are masters of many of London's showpiece royal events: the controllers and staff of the Lord Chamberlian's office, who are unerring professional courtiers and, in my experience, the most industrious and suavely efficient arrangers of state happenings in the world.

Princess Anne's wedding day, in short, was one national pageant *not* organized by the man who for so long had been the grand master of such things: the Duke of Norfolk. But he was present in the Abbey, this Bernard Marmaduke FitzAlan Howard, Hereditary Marshal and Chief Butler of England, the country's Premier Duke and Earl. He was there as personal guest and friend of the Royal Family he had served as long as most of them could remember. As he sat, English as an oak, in the forefront of the congregation, and watched with those heavy-lidded eyes the dignity of the processions, his mind must have travelled back over the decades of his own stage-managing of great occasions – coronations, royal processions, the Investiture of the Prince of Wales. He was feeling his years now, relinquishing some of his duties, even his racing activities: in the past year he had acted as Sovereign's Representative at Ascot for the last time after twenty-seven meticulous years. He would not have a hand in a State Opening of Parliament again. He had little more than a year to live. . . .

Because I recalled that last appearance of his, in the Abbey, on the day he died – and because my experiences on *that* day were another example of how news broadcasting works – perhaps it is not malapropos to end this chapter with an account of 31 January 1975.

At eight-thirty that morning I was just sitting down, rather blear-eyed, to breakfast in a small hotel in Staffordshire, where I had been lecturing the night before, when the girl from the hall desk ran into the dining room to say I was wanted urgently on the telephone. It was a BBC news editor in London to say that the Duke of Norfolk was dead – a flash had come in a few minutes ago – and, as I had known him, could I do a little tribute? Could I moreover do it now, straight off, on the the phone: they were ready to connect the call directly into the 'Today' programme. I said I supposed I must try. While I was being given a black coffee and a few seconds to think, the second telephone on the hotel desk rang: 'Godfrey Talbot? Independent Radio News here: LBC. Can you possibly do us a piece on the Earl Marshal? We can put you on the air at once from this telephone – it's a good line.'

So both sides had ferreted me out!

To say that the next ten minutes were busy is an understatement. Both callers got an appreciation and a short biography of His Grace – or at least they got the best I could do without notes and without time to collect wits and words. I spoke the pieces whilst leaning weakly over the counter of the unorthodox 'studio' under the unbelieving stare of the little hotel receptionist who stood watching a strange broadcasting performance. She was not too dumbfounded at my goings-on, however, to shush three commercial travellers who, puzzled and ill pleased, had to stand waiting to pay their bills until I had finished.

The two unpremeditated breakfast-time talks were only the beginning of a hectic day. When I got back to London, other programme producers were waiting; and in the next few hours I was interviewed at the microphone and spoke on television half a dozen times. I was in and out of studios and taxis, in and out of Television Centre at White City and the old film studios at Lime Grove where the BBC still runs TV Current Affairs. All the time giving memories of Bernard Norfolk. The man who in his lifetime had been a master showman and yet had shied from the spotlight himself, was widely publicized in death. Rightly. He was one of the characters of our time. His passing was a sadness, but I was glad to be asked to recall the flavour of the man.

He was a prime example of the old landed gentry with a sense of public duty and a talent for administration, a man of quiet civilized distinction, and of loyalty and kindness and fun – and one who dissembled those qualities under a mask of taciturnity and aloofness. It was the Australians who publicly unearthed his salty wit and good companionship after someone at Lord's in 1962 had the inspired thought to send him Down Under as manager of the MCC touring team, business man as well as cricket lover. He was a success with the Aussies, and he at once warmed to them too. 'Dookie', they called him; and he liked it. The stuffier backwaters of Official London – who knew only the caustic Master of Ceremonies, the stickler who at the Churchill funeral had grunted that 'we were full two minutes late at St Paul's' – would have been astonished at the way their Earl Marshal unbent in the rough and tumble of Sydney and Brisbane. But it was not surprising to the friends who knew him, for instance, as a raconteur. I never heard anybody tell such hilarious stories while maintaining an absolute boot face. There was no highfalutin' nonsense about him. I was interviewing him one day, and asked what his title, 'Chief Butler of England', really meant. A rare chuckle came out as he said: 'You know, I've never actually found out. Nobody's ever asked me to do any butlering. At coronation banquets long ago I believe they used to give the Earl Marshal a loving-cup after he'd handed the thing round. But I've never been given one. Wish I had. Anyhow, let's not be dogmatic about my job – except that I don't buttle. But I do a few other things besides ceremonies, you know. I enjoy being with my family here at Arundel.'

It was at his Castle of Arundel in Sussex, deep in the vault, that they laid the sixteenth Duke to rest, widely mourned. He was sixty-six. His funeral day was the twenty-third anniversary of the accession to the throne of the Queen he had officially proclaimed and diligently attended. His passing was a loss, not because of his pages in *Debrett*, and not only because he was a Great Officer of State, but because of the sort of person he was. With him an era was over, a kingpost of the old country gone. I saw him, in the pageant of the years I have known, as a Hereward, last of the English.

It is difficult to find leaders and patriots now. It is difficult to find England and the English. We are so cursed by trendy wreckers of tradition and loyalty, so invaded and infiltrated by alien people and foreign ways, that our motherland is in danger of becoming an abstraction and pride of country something to apologize for. Meanwhile we are governed by computers, not men.

And if the nation has taken a beating, so has its tongue. Nasty things have happened to the English language. Yet spoken English, my business, has been enriched as well as eroded. Word-broadcasting has become a universal weapon and a way of life in my time.

14

Words, Words, Words

Adolf Hitler and Winston Churchill, protagonists of the first great war of the Broadcasting Age, used radio to the full and with skill, the one for evil and the other for good. The Nazis during the euphoria of their septic thirties were quick to recognize the power of the wireless, and they made sure that not only the Führer's rabble-rousing rantings but all the cheers and drums and ecstatic descriptions of the Brownshirts' marches and rallies were sent throbbing into the air from every German broadcasting station. Without public radio, without their cunning exploitation of it to appeal unscrupulously to mass emotions, Hitler and his adherents could not have gained so swiftly and surely their ascendancy and backing in the Fatherland and their fatal stranglehold on the surrounding peoples. When war came and Hitler's armies surged through Europe and aimed for world conquest, the German ether was totally enslaved and bound to the military chariot. Radio was the muscle and might of the Goebbels propaganda arm. Germany's wartime broadcasts, unsubtle though the messages often were in their lies and in their messages directed at Britain and the free world, had the strength of wide dissemination and the coercion that comes of loud repetition.

Churchill and the British used the medium more intelligently than their enemies did, but its most memorable use was by Churchill personally, as a soloist and star performer. His voice was one of our greatest weapons. With him there was no resort to bands and bombast, no threats and false promises. He simply talked, and the sound of him went intimately into the homes of the world. He employed forthright, robust old words; and the merit of it was that he could be believed because he told the plain truth, whether the tidings he had to broadcast were heartening or harsh. He recited the odds piled against us – and then inspired great confidence against those odds. With all his classic majesty of language, he sat at the microphone and mobilized the English tongue and sent it into battle. It was 'on the broadcast' that he publicly charted the course that won the war. And Britain became, in those years, the greatest broadcasting power in the world.

All that was almost a lifetime ago. Since those days – days of Sound radio only – television, as the prime medium of information, has come to be a chief weapon of those who exercise influence and power; it is the big stick which politicians wield. Today's traffic in pictures-by-wireless almost swamps the other media; and in the last thirty years careers have been made and broken, causes won and lost, by personal performances on the little screen. A statesman's rise is boosted, or his downfall precipitated, by his electromagnetic image. Moreover the Box is not only the strongest arm and swiftest arbiter in the communications business: it sometimes also seems an end as well as a means, truer than truth, realler than real, gospel as well as gloss. To the idle and impressionable viewer, unstirring in his armchair, TV can become an escape from first-hand experience and a substitute for life itself.

Yet there is no television take-over. Sound radio today still marches – indeed, marches with reborn vigour – beside Big Brother Vision. Radio not only remains, but has been reconfirmed as the most widespread instant-communicator, far from destroyed by the television explosion. It penetrates everywhere, available and used all the time.

They once said that the telly would kill the radio, just as they had said that radio would kill gramophone records. What nonsenses those prognostications proved to be! It is true that when TV was blossoming into the new Wonder of the World we thought it might possibly be the very incubus and annihilator of 'steam radio', for it threatened to turn Sound into an old-fashioned minority medium, mere 'broadcasting for the blind'. But not a bit of it! After a few years the novelty of television, marvellous though certain peak programmes were, began to wear thin, and its output was often a time-consuming yawn. Then, in the last ten years, while that mild disenchantment was spreading, radio has received a new lease of life from the tremendous proliferation of small transistorized receivers and car radios. It has become so easy and so convenient to listen; and the quality of reception has improved so much Radio, in short, has come back, brisk and bouncy, the liveliest and most immediate source of information wherever you go. And the cheapest too: there is now no licence fee for Sound.

In news-broadcasting, the senders of the programmes have benefited from technical advances just as the receivers have. Recording gear and microphones have become less cumbersome and much more mobile. It has become easier to transmit voice reports and to edit tapes; and this has helped radio news to be speedy and smart as never before.

The vocal manner of radio's newsmen has become newly brisk and trenchant too. A new style developed with the coming to the microphone in 1965 of the late William Hardcastle, who for ten years until his death in 1975 was the chief presenter of the Radio Four programmes 'The World at One' and 'PM', the archetype of the new era of British radio journalism. Bill was no golden voice, indeed was far from the clearest of speakers. He gabbled breathlessly and was often uncomfortably brusque and tough as he sought to dig the truth out of the people he interviewed. But in fact he was likeable, good tempered and fair – the complete professional with a wholehearted zest for news. He and his followers revitalized radio reporting and interviewing, and made 'The World at One' a programme with a big audience and a big prestige. Cabinet ministers gladly jumped into their cars and sped to Broadcasting House when the Hardcastle voice came on the telephone and invited them to come in and be interviewed. Newspaper offices still tape-record 'The World at One' every day to check on the stories and the follow-ups they have missed. And in millions of British homes the radio is switched on between one and one-thirty with absolute regularity.

'The World at One' epitomizes the modern News Division style, probing and abrasive, bustling with its stories and rough with its contributors. It is superficial and bitty, its speakers jerk and slur. It cocks snooks at national Authority and at BBC Establishment as well, unhesitatingly breaking old Corporation conventions and giving the disrespectful 'Young Turks' of Portland Place their head. Within the BBC, as well as among the listeners, the programme, though closely listened-to, is not everybody's darling. But it is everybody's programme: everybody and everything is admitted – except a BBC accent.

For that matter, radio broadcasting in general has become everybody's thing. No longer do the professional talkers and the political pundits dominate the output. At almost any hour there are phone-in programmes on the air, bringing to listeners the sound of their fellows, the voices of ordinary members of the public arguing with experts or simply riding their own hobby-horses. To have a go yourself at one of these tangles you do not have to trek to a studio: you simply lift a telephone and call. Such programmes have an attractive rawness and spontaneity; they are slices of life, budgets of advice, outlets for anger, feats of frustration and fun. Commercial stations have embraced them with ardour, of course: they cost hardly anything, for you do not pay the contributors, and indeed it is they who provide the programme ideas. Ready-made stuff. So we have 'Open Line' and 'Nightline' and 'Grapevine' and the rest, thickly sprinkled in the schedules. Every night is amateur night.

The BBC is not far behind, with its free forums like 'Voice of the People' and 'Tuesday Call' and 'It's Your Line'. All that and the free broadcasting of Parliament too. Radio is the voice of the people indeed; plebs as well as prime ministers are in the talking business.

The process, to be sure, began during the war when talks that were unscripted were first allowed to permeate the programmes as part of a deliberate policy of relaxing listeners' tensions and bringing the warmth of natural voices, however rough-hewn, into the homes of an anxious and harassed people.

But, unfortunately, the process has now gone so far that clear and civilized speech is by no means always easy to find:

the air is thick with the chatter of adenoidal amateurs doing their best to kick spoken English to death. People without wisdom or knowledge or articulation. If I were using their language to comment on the change that has come about I would say: 'Honest, we definitely didn't used to yak like they natter on like now.'

It is not only the amateurs who offend. Professionals, and so-called professionals, of radio are also guilty of butchering the words and torturing the ear so that comprehension is made difficult. Perhaps this is because there are so many of them, with no time for training (in any case, you cannot train people who normally speak badly, and, alas, the BBC nowadays does employ some people *as talkers* whose natural speech is quite dreadful). Perhaps it is the slipshod chatter of the guests in a programme, or the low standards of talk on some local radio stations, which rubs off on the staff speakers who should be setting an example. Perhaps it is simply because there are no exams, no 'A' Levels, no professional degree courses in the business – because, in short, anybody can say, if he comes stuttering on the air often enough, 'I am a broadcaster'. Whatever the reason, some of the regulars do jar the ear with distressing regularity.

Even one or two of the news-readers are infected. There are still some, praise be, who patently have been educated, have some experience of life, and have learned how words are pronounced; and these men – a few excellent women too nowadays – remain as models of clarity and of civilized, understandable speech; but the other kind are unpleasant in sound and – this is the sad thing – not easy to follow.

The best speech to be heard on the radio comes from the announcers who broadcast in the English transmissions of the BBC World Service for listeners overseas (though you can receive these broadcasts in the United Kingdom); next best are the voices of the domestic Radio Three; close behind comes Radio Four; but on Radio Two you may or may not get someone easy on the ear – there are days on that channel, and certainly on jangling Radio One, when you suspect that there must be a competition in progress to see who can mispronounce the most words.

Admittedly it is not easy to keep your standards when all about you are losing theirs, braying and blethering, peppering their utterances with pitiful 'you knows' and 'sort ofs', and talking about 'dee-fects' and 'ree-search' and 'droring' conclusions from something which is a 'mute' point. American verbosity is aped as the speakers tell how they have 'met up with' such-and-such, or how they sadly are 'missing out' on something 'at this moment of time'. As to tautology, in one week I heard 'plummeted down' and 'a hollow tube' and 'a foot pedal'. Some of this stuff, it is true, comes from chat-show chairmen, but too much of it is uttered by certain of the staff men and reporters. Which is sinful, for news cannot afford to be complicated by distorted utterance.

The trouble is that the line between broadcasting and show biz-talk, which thrives on quirks, is getting pretty blurred.

I can readily forgive the man who genuinely hasn't come across, say, the names of Wriothesley and Featherstonehaugh, and hasn't had time to look them up and discover that these surnames are said as 'Roxley' and 'Fanshaw' (or, just as correctly, it could be 'Feeson-hay' or half a dozen other alternatives). I understand perfectly that an equerry, an officer in personal attendance upon a royal personage, can properly be called an '*ekk*-werrie' or may equally properly be pronounced the other way – which I have always adopted, ever since the day when King George the Sixth personally picked up a telephone and rang the BBC News Room and said: 'Will you tell your announcer that the word is "ek-*werrie*" with the accent on the second syllable.' But those are proper and special names, and you sometimes have to choose from a number of alternative sounds. Quite different, and quite unforgivable, is mispronouncing everyday words – for this not only annoys the educated listener but gets in the way of understanding.

I received a letter not long ago from an old friend, an honest seeker after information. Here's a bit of the letter: 'Is anything being done to combat the raging infection of transatlantic gobbledygook which uses six words instead of one? Why *is* the foreigner, in the World Service, addressed in well-said, straightforward English while the British at home are often given chancy, sloppy stuff full of words grotesquely misused? What in the name of glory *is* the pronounciation policy of the BBC?'

My friend was flying off the handle a bit in that letter; and when questions of that kind are put squarely, I must in all fairness turn – not devil's advocate but, for a moment, counsel for the defence. Because it is not for want of BBC trying that standards have fallen – and the sheer volume of news-talking nowadays makes schooling and careful preparation difficult. It is not accidental, moreover, that speech is more careful and more clear in broadcasting to overseas audiences: the fact is that such transmissions have to run the gauntlet, even in this day, of short-wave fading and crackling. Consequently, the World Service announcer must take special trouble to ensure that at any rate the words are good and pure when they leave his mouth. There is also, I must say, an admirable pride in language at Bush House, which is where the External Services live.

Though it may be hard to credit, there still exists a BBC Pronunciation Unit: it is a small but excellent one and is located in Broadcasting House. It is there to be consulted; it is at the disposal of the whole Corporation. And such pronunciation guidance as is given by the BBC to its servants is precisely the same for all three output Directorates – Television, Radio and External Services.

The Pronunciation Unit has a card-index of 100,000 entries, a small staff and a highly qualified lady in charge who bears the appropriate name of Mrs Wright. The unit has grown out of the Advisory Committee on Spoken English which John Reith set up in a year of national emergency, the General Strike year of 1926, and it has existed in its present form ever since a year of far wider peril, the war's outbreak year of 1939. Its rulings are mandatory for staff announcers and newsreaders, and it is hoped always that the rulings will be sought or brought to the attention of reporters and outside contributors to programmes. No more than that: a pious hope. In fact, the reporters and the rest rarely use the Unit.

That is a pity. The Unit's guidance is not only helpful but is also highly sympathetic to the changes which must happen to a living language. It deals in decent speech but is not dogmatic or dated. They realize, those ladies of Pronunciation, that though the pioneer staff speakers – Hibberd and Grisewood, Lidell and Phillips – set a first-class standard of intelligibility, the style of the thirties does seem a little bit like oral print now; they allow that conversational stresses and some colloquialisms are an understood part of the speech of the seventies. They do not insist on one uniform spoken language, but they do purvey common denominators – in the hope that they will prevent speech fashions from becoming speech faults.

John Reith was surprisingly tolerant on this point. The stern D-G who has gone down in history as an authoritarian who imposed a rigid and old-fashioned will upon the Corporation's output, never laid down the law about the sound of words. He held that spoken language is what people actually say as opposed to what some may think they should say. He went so far as to declare that in language 'there are no experts, only users'. All the same, he always wanted good, authoritative speech from the users of his studios.

Today, the users of the air are legion. So it is not easy for listeners, especially listeners seeking to lay blame, to distinguish between the 'official voice' of the announcer and all the other fast-working specialist talkers whose accents are not, and cannot be, supervised – and are by no means always a joy to hear.

It is difficult, for that matter, for the laymen to distinguish between the two principal kinds of Current Affairs broadcasting (which have been my own kinds): news-reporting and giving running commentaries. The reporter generally provides short, factual stories for bulletins and news programmes; the commentator is one who, on the spot and usually 'live', describes at length a scene or an event of importance or public interest. The business of giving a commentary is not so frenetic as the reporter's practice; but it is greater in scope, in personal responsibility, in preparation, in the demands it makes on the performer – and in pitfalls. It is not usual for one broadcaster to be both reporter and commentator, specialist correspondent too. I have therefore been fortunate, in my BBC career, to have escaped type-casting, to have been a worker in those several fields, and in particular to have had a foot in two very different – sometimes mutually suspicious and even competing – camps: News Division and Outside Broadcasts. I have always enjoyed my stints for OBs, the department of commentators.

A commentator! The voice you hear on big occasions! The public's notion of the man and the job has glamour and charisma about it, partly perhaps because there are few of this kind of broadcaster, whereas reporters are numerous. How do you become a commentator? I am often asked this when I am lecturing – and I can never give a crisp and satisfying reply. For there is no royal road to success, no school or correspondence course which can make a good performer of the scriptless spontaneous descriptive job. You cannot turn the wrong sort of man into the right sort of commentator. OB communicators are born rather than made. But you do learn as you go along; you discover a lot of basic do's and don'ts. Years ago, the BBC printed a leaflet titled 'Notes for Would-be Commentators', which sagely asked the would-be's to test themselves severely before seeking an audition, and listed some essentials for good commentary. When I look at those old notes and relate them to modern conditions and my own experience of making mistakes in public, a few rules and principles emerge. I have listed some of them. They are really, of course, tips for those 'in the trade' or hoping to be so. But maybe they do give a useful inkling of a broadcaster's problems:

Before you start, possess and understand a stopwatch. Timing is all.

Whilst his particular OB is on the air, the commentator should never stop looking closely at the scene, even when some participant in that scene is doing the speaking, and even when the broadcast is consisting simply of 'clean sound' of, say, the military band on the spot. Be ready to break in if an unexpected occurrence makes an explanatory word from you necessary.

If you are commentating on television, keep one eye on your monitor screen as well as looking at the actual scene in front of you. Because you must know what picture your producer is transmitting to the viewers at any given moment (he will always have several camera shots to choose from) so that any words you say are related to what the viewer at home is looking at. The picture the viewer is getting may be out of your view if the scene before you is changing fast. (Once, at a march-past, I spoke of the splendid sight a Gloucesters' colonel was making as he marched before us, but at that moment the viewers at their TV sets were beholding the march of a Welsh regiment's mascot goat.)

Let the pictures themselves tell the story whenever possible, without you chipping in.

The thing to remember is that what the viewer at home sees has a much greater impact than what he hears (just as, in the News, half the customers hardly remember what the announcer has just said, but they all know what his necktie was like and whether it was straight). So – talk only when something needs identifying or clarifying. Anticipate and answer the queries which may be arising in viewers' minds because of something they are looking at.

As commentator, you are the servant of the picture, supplementing it with a few words when that is desirable. You are an annotator.

Example. When the viewers are seeing the Prime Minister walking along – just as clearly as you are seeing him – it is gratuitously annoying to say 'There goes the PM walking up the steps.' But if a little-known person comes prominently into view on the screen, then it is your business to know who it is and to say who it is.

Prepare mightily before the day of the commentary – and attend any rehearsal there may be. You cannot soak in too many facts and too much history (so long as you don't, on the day, air your homework for the sake of it!).

Swot-up the public and the personal history of the chief actors in the ceremony and be ready to pop in an occasional ten-word character sketch.

Have at hand plenty of associative material – about earlier events, surrounding buildings, precedents and personalities – but when you use the material weave it in bit by bit so that it comes smoothly into the continuous descriptive story according to whatever is happening. Never spill it out, that is, in sudden great wodges, as though you were reading a catalogue in the studio. Remember that you are a man on the spot, where the action is, reacting to that action.

A telling beginning and a neat ending are important to your broadcast: no harm whatever in having *those* roughed-out and ready in advance.

Never, never read from a script. But do have notes: if you've written points down on a bit of paper you've probably written them on your memory too, so the more you've done your homework the less you will need to keep looking at notes. Most of the experienced commentators have with them a collection of headings on small white cards, easily shuffled.

Be informal, not pompous. An occasional light touch even on solemn occasions is welcome. But don't let what *you* think is funny run away with you. You are only an agent serving the ears and eyes of listeners and viewers. Don't obtrude yourself.

Don't orate or lecture. Broadcasting is an intimate and very personal means of communication. Remember that you are speaking to somebody sitting in the lounge at home, or maybe drying the dishes, or at the wheel of a car with the radio on. You are not addressing the nation: speak as though chatting to one person or one family. Your audience will number millions, but they are listening as individuals, probably alone, not *as* a vast audience.

Most of this advice applies to speaking on both television and radio. When you are speaking on radio only, it is important to let the 'effects' talk for themselves – the cheers, the music, the speeches, the jingle and clatter of horse-carriages and cavalry.

Give an occasional bit of fine-focus detail rather than labouring over an attempt to describe a whole big scene. For example, give a quick *impression* of place and atmosphere with a word-picture of one drooping flag, the actions of one policeman, the face of one child among many, or the clothes and the gestures of one old lady in the crowd. Scenes come to life by such close-ups.

Have a few good phrases prepared on your crib-cards, perhaps, but don't ever read out whole sentences which you have rehearsed and polished. Pronouncements in glossy, inflexible grammar are not wanted: they make the listener have to strain to follow you. Be yourself, an impressionable human being on the spot, not a grandiose guide-book. A fairly conversational style is best.

Above all, a commentator should sound to be a pleasant, ordinary chap, observant and dependable and well-informed, but not a pundit. Educated and articulate, yes, but not above putting a word wrong now and then: a slight slip very occasionally could even establish a bond between you and the person hearing you, for the listener will think: 'After all, he's a fallible human being like me.'

Try not to be upset if you hear yourself make a mistake: probably it sounded worse to you than it really was – and half the listeners won't have noticed it anyway.

Say what you want to say with confidence: don't be apologetic or tentative – and neither hoity-toity nor hesitant. Certainly you shouldn't offend the Oxford don, but don't upstage the Hoxton dustman either!

. . . It is easy to give advice, of course. I hope my suggestions don't scare the daylights out of people thinking of having a go at spontaneous description. They should not really be frightened, for – as I see when I read over my list – I have ricocheted between counsel of perfection and blinding glimpse of the obvious. At any rate, such are the hints I might offer to young aspirants in this particular branch of the talking business. They may arouse public sympathy for commentators.

They may also arouse the scorn of some people who are in the trade: one or two of the new generation of news broadcasters, prickly about being given advice by anybody who began in Reithian radio. I do not mind that: they are perhaps making their own golden age. What I do mind is the tendency to deride established practice, not necessarily because it has been found wanting but simply because it exists. Disparaging is fashionable. Reputations are made in broadcasting nowadays not by any manifest respect for elders or for order or tradition, but by being cynical about the past, careless about standards and rude to authority. Youngsters with no experience and no manners are seen to thrive. Their motto might be: 'What can we tear apart today?' Butchery to make a newsroom holiday. On with the clever talk!

That is a pessimistic view – confounded to some extent, I have to admit, by the existence of a few skilful and polished performers at the microphone. But in my darker moments I have wondered just how useful the present-day mass of topical broadcasting is; how beneficial the extended bulletins and the almost incessant programmes which detail and explore the events of the hour. Is it necessary to have the dire scenes of lawlessness so prominently displayed in television news ('If it's grim, they'll bare it', someone said of the news-film editors)? Is it possible that all the dolorous speculation on bad news which we get day after day is an aggravation of the world's ills? Could we not well do without it? Would it perhaps help mankind if there were to be a cut-back on current affairs coverage, so as to let only the bare facts circulate? Should we not try having merely half a dozen crisp and brief bulletins each twenty-four hours – the news unembroidered by sensational film, by the misery of 'experts', cross-talk acts in the studios and Mickey Mouse-voice elaborations by distant reporters over indifferent telephone lines? What about some censorship – of taste and verbosity? And, for another thing, cannot we have some news-reporting of life's *quiet* things and beneficial achievements? Why does it seem that always the bad news, hardly ever a bit of good news, fills the bulletins?

But having put those queries, and thought about them for a moment, I also know what the answers are. To start with, to take up that last point about not giving *good* news (such as world records in British coal production and running British railway trains), the fact is that such items may get into a bulletin if they can fight their way in as part of a, say, ten-minute round-up of news informing society about itself at that time. But if there are a lot of sharply new and different things to report, then the items could get crowded out: a news editor's business is not to put in news with the aim of cheering people up. He can only *hope* that, in an objective choosing of items making up a general picture, bits of good news will get in. News, by definition, is things that are out of the ordinary. So, because much of life is constructive and good, news is usually distressing.

The Chairman of the Governors of the BBC, Sir Michael Swann, has put this point well in saying: 'If virtually every train on British Rail crashed with loss of life, then we should of course automatically report the arrival of the odd one safe and sound at its destination – we would report it with a fanfare. But the fact is that trains seldom crash, buildings seldom fall down, people seldom go in for murder and kidnapping and most of the time most people are at work and not on strike; so that it makes no sense to report these admirable norms every day.'

As to the constant detailed flow of news, the truth is that it is proper, it is useful, and it must stay. It is a full service *offered*: you do not *have* to take it. All the news must be there, *available when wanted*.

To reply to the rest of my own questions: however much

news-indigestion we may get, draconian rationing of output would be retrograde idiocy. The rationing should be done at the intake end of broadcasting – in the home, at the switch-off knob of the television receiver and the transistor set. It is up to the *user* of information to take what he wants from the full information provided and, it must be hoped, to make his own judgements on it. An informed people *must* be a better people. To cut down information would be to increase misunderstanding.

And, in addition to news, the direct broadcasting of great events is surely more than worth while too. The world would be even more miserable than it is if we were not able to be transported at times, by word and picture, direct to spectacular and sporting occasions, watching and listening to happier and statelier events than the grim and squalid happenings which so often make the day's news.

Broadcasting has rightly become a requisite of modern life. Auntie, now well over half a century old, the Auntie BBC who took over my own professional life away back in 1937, is very much here to stay and is the dominant figure of the ether, however young and smart the new Commercial Uncle may be. The arrival of Uncle, indeed, did Auntie a power of good inasmuch as he made her realize that monopoly is soporific and competition stimulating. Auntie can't do just as she likes nowadays. She must, for one thing, woo as well as waylay the public; she must chase audiences. No use putting on programmes if the audience has fled.

So the BBC today is an entertainment empire and an information factory, no longer an Establishment focus and an arbiter of taste. It still bestows patronage and temporary status, but not grace and style. Sometimes it lets inquiry become inquisition, and realism rudeness, because it has grown up in a brusque society. The BBC used to fashion public behaviour but now follows it.

Much of the change has been inevitable, since Auntie – now saddled with a nasty name, The Beeb – is no longer so special but is one of a number of large communicators-by-wireless, and, like others, has to fight for life. Not a bad thing in some ways, because in the struggle she has got rid of some dull fat and developed diverting fizz. The old firm has become a bigger deployer of talent than ever and, stimulated by challenge, often more professional and businesslike than its sleek commercial rivals. Also stronger than ever. Through all the great changes which the fifty years have brought, the BBC's lasting achievement is that all the time it has resisted governmental and political attempts at take-over. It is still an independent, public-service corporation and not a state broadcasting department (the name Independent is used to describe the commercial concerns but is a misnomer, for they are dependent on advertising).

As a field worker in broadcasting, I have been witness and beneficiary of marvellous developments in technical operation and editorial slickness. Responsibility has been spread, team-work has become the key. The cameraman, the tape-cutter and the film editor are, in the field of news, arbiters every bit as powerful as the reporter; they are together as much a force for good or ill as the men who use the microphone in radio and put words to pictures in television. All are communicators now. All stars – or all chorus.

There has been a levelling of microphone performance: hundreds of word-users are at work, probing, debunking, synthesizing. Very few news-talkers are outstanding.

Gone are the days of the broadcasting reporter who was a towering individual, clean above the rest. No Richard Dimbleby now, no one man indispensably seen and heard in a whole range of outlets. The circumstances are different; the streams of talk and film have become oceans, and afloat on them are today's hordes of eager, generally fairly competent and usable reporters, instruments of the great information machine. It is not an unmerited aspersion to say that the majority, though named, stay anonymous – and undistinguished in the manner in which they speak English. There won't ever be another Richard Dimbleby. It wouldn't be allowed to happen. Some animals must *not* be more equal than others.

This is not to say that the commentator's day is done. And certainly not the reporter's day. On the contrary. The news-reader is essential too, in television as well as radio: every picture tells a story, but unexplained pictures would be irritating, often meaningless and worse. To run the TV 'Nine o'Clock News' or 'News at Ten' in silence, with the film flickering away mute and uncaptioned, would be disastrous. The power and omnipresence of television picture information, the impact of its news, the universal audience, the awful responsibility of the Box, its capacity for affecting decisions and influencing events – all this demands the accompaniment of the spoken word, judicious and accurate, to point and interpret the fleeting clips of news-film. Without the News Room's speech, the pictures, which in the nature of the inescapable editorial processes are selective and fragmentary, are wide open to misunderstanding. The image needs the word balance, for context, for perspective. So the sub-editors and the news-readers are necessary.

My particular world has been the world of the other sort of talkers – the commentators, the correspondents, the reporters who have to be versatile and are not lost without a script. This kind of broadcaster must be an individual as well as an instrument, demonstrably a human person for all his impartiality. He speaks words which are his own rather than typed out by others for him to read. Exemplars are lively people like Raymond Baxter, Robert Hudson, Robin Day, Jonathan Dimbleby (one of Richard's sons), Martin Bell, Gerald Priestland and Charles Wheeler. The established masters. They are the sort who, at any hour of day or night and anywhere in the world, are required to jump into action with manly ardour and sacred joy as the news whip cracks and the story breaks, to tell their tale swiftly and succinctly, and to speak it well.

And the best of them *do* speak well. You don't catch the top-sawyers, the professionals, sounding sloppy or don't-care, overwrought or lack-lustre – as the slipshod second-raters so lamentably do.

One thing, however, I have no reservations about. Good, bad and indifferent, all of them enjoy the job. I have never come across anybody in my business of itinerant news broadcaster who really didn't like it, slog though it often is. None of them has been pressed into it; they have worked and waited and wangled to become appointed. They never voluntarily leave the work. Their idea of hell is a safe, steady job that guarantees your commuting to suburbia at half past five every night. Their heaven is odd hours, hard labour, and heavy pressure when the rest of the world is asleep, an inverted existence. For them, journalism is a thing of going off and leaving the wife and bairns you love, because you love chasing a news story almost as much. The news assignment is an escape, an excuse, a savoured divertimento. You would hate to be without your unusual life – and your 'unsocial hours', far from being something to go on strike about, are a treasured part of it.

Among the new generation of such adventurers in broad-casting, some noticeably first-class hands are beginning to be discernible. And what a joy it is when they are heard! Perceptive and quick, they have pleasant but unobtrusive person-alities; and plainly they have been the recipients of education: their speech gives neither strain nor offence. Surfacing from any day's sea of glue-worded mediocrity, above the ruck, they are increasingly to be seen and heard – for the simple reason that obvious talent becomes much employed. They have got to know and to respect the microphone, which at first is your master, then your mistress, then your matchless servant. With them the future of the profession is bright after all, however melancholy the news which they will surely have to tell in the years ahead. They have already earned their Grade One – and my salute, my regard, my envy. They are enjoying that per-mission to speak which for so long has happily informed my own life.

Lucky chaps! The world's their oyster.

Index